FROM THE
CRADLE
TO THE
STAGE

FROM THE CRADLE TO THE STAGE

ALAN SWAN

POOLBEG

Published 2003
by Poolbeg Press Ltd
123 Grange Hill, Baldoyle
Dublin 13, Ireland
E-mail: poolbeg@poolbeg.com

Typesetting, layout, design © Poolbeg Group Services Ltd.

1 3 5 7 9 10 8 6 4 2

A catalogue record for this book is available from the British Library.

ISBN 1-84223-164-2

Typeset by Magpie Designs in Palatino 11.5/15.8
Printed by CPD Group, Wales

www.poolbeg.com

ABOUT THE AUTHOR

Born in Co. Kildare, Alan Swan is one of Ireland's most talented young broadcasters. As *The Breakfast Show* producer and presenter with *CKRFM*, Alan won a new Irish Music Industry award in recognition of his encouragement of new talent in Ireland. As a student at NUI Maynooth, Alan set up the university's first temporary radio station. The following year a further temporary license was awarded by the Broadcasting Commission of Ireland. As a result Alan was presented with the AIB "Endeavour Award" for outstanding achievement. More recently, Alan has presented *ID* on Network 2 and RTE1's legendary *The Den.*

Now 24 years of age, Alan is currently the music researcher for RTE/Tyrone Productions *Open House.*

ACKNOWLEDGEMENTS

A project as time-consuming as this one could not have been completed without the help of some wonderfully talented and passionate people. Firstly my appreciation must go to *Hot Press* writer Jackie Hayden who served as my editor on this book. He must have been sick of my name appearing on his e-mail in-box. Jackie, you must have the patience of a saint. Thank you for all the advice and the encouragement you brought to this project.

To the wonderful staff at Fighting Blindness, especially Eamonn Carroll and Michael Griffith, who continue to work tirelessly to help over 65,000 people who suffer from Retinal Degenerative Diseases. Their work is an inspiration to others.

To Paula, Sarah, Lynda, Georgina, Anne, Brona, Dave, Kieran and all the staff at Poolbeg (publishers supreme), and whose positive support made writing this book such a real joy. Thank you all for having so much faith in this book and in my ability.

To the many musicians and singers who appear in this book, thank you for so generously taking the time from your already busy schedules to answer my questions. Please keep doing what you all do best, bringing entertainment and inspiration to so many. To those we couldn't include in this book, here's to Volume uimhear a dó!

To the many record, management and public relations companies who helped organise the interviews. To all of you, a heartfelt thanks! Special mention goes to Martin Byrne, Dan and Lisa @ Friction; Niamh Burkeneff @ NB; Maire Claire and Janet @ Sony; Lindsey, Deirdre and Sinead @ LHP; Colm @ Verge; Anne and Kathryn @ Universal; Stephen @ BMG; Pete and Gill @ EMI; Louis Walsh and Flo Irwin, Yvonne @ Rosette, Juliet @ Hummingbird; Sorcha O'Flanagan, Derek Nally, Felib

rbonell, Bernie and Robert @ Treasure Island; Ailish
Toohey, Liz Devlin, Mike Hanrahan, Mim Scala, Stevo
Berube, Dennis O'Reilly, Ciara Gaynor and Mike @ Schism
PR; Mattie Fox Management, Gearóid McIntyre, Catherine
and Leah @ Warner; Sabrina Sheehan, Gerry Browne, Des
Ekin, Michael Doherty, Stuart Clarke, Luka Bloom, Jedda
Downey, Turloch, Jane and Anita @ Wonderland; Tom
Sherlock, Barry Gastor, Brian Allen, Connie Lynch, Shane
McDonnell, Carol & Associates, Barbara Galavan, Linda
Martin and Seamus Casey.

To Gay Byrne for taking the time to provide this project
with its graceful and thought-provoking foreword. Thank
you, Gay.

To the staff and management of CKRFM, especially Terry
Martin, for use of the facilities in CKR. Cheers, lads! To my
colleagues in RTE, especially in the Young People's
Department, thank you also for your encouragement.

A personal thank-you to all my relatives and friends who
endured me (or had no chance to endure me!) between
March of 2002 and August of 2003. Especially Mairéad
Cashin and Dave McGrath, two brilliant friends who have
never let me down. A1 Players both.

Finally, to my parents, Michael and Josephine Swan.
Thank you both for always letting me do what I've loved
doing and for supporting me through thick and thin. You
have always been so positive about all the things that I do,
and I will never forget how good you are to me.

This book has been a pleasure to put together. Of course
there have been late nights, brick walls to surmount, faxes
here and e-mails there, interviews in the morning, interviews at the weekend, interviews at some very strange
times I barely knew existed, many an argument and many
a headache but it's all been worth it. Many thanks for
buying a copy and in turn helping Fighting Blindness. I
hope you enjoy reading the stories as much as I have
enjoyed compiling them.

Alan Swan - August 2003

INTRODUCTION

In the past few decades Irish music has made an extraordinary impact all around the world and it is not unusual to hear the music of Irish musicians while waiting in airports or train stations in any part of Europe, the US or even as far away as Japan and Australia. The extraordinary success of Irish musicians is not only a source of great pride to all of us but has helped to profile our country internationally which in turn benefits us in many different ways both directly from tourism and indirectly by creating the right atmosphere for attracting inward investment. The impact of the international success of Irish music is difficult to overstate.

It is timely, therefore, that this chronicle of the stories of leading Irish musicians of the past thirty to forty years should be brought into the public domain. It is a great credit to author Alan Swan and all the musicians who have co-operated in the production of this volume that they have chosen to do this in such a way that this history of the Irish music industry will also be an extraordinary help to one of Ireland's leading research charities, Fighting Blindness.

Fighting Blindness has been in existence for the past twenty years and in itself has achieved international success through its research programmes in over half-a-dozen institutes around the country. Its flagship project in Trinity College is a world leader in the development of gene therapy for dominantly inherited retinopathies, and the contribution of this group to the global research effort to find treatments for blindness has been truly outstanding by international terms.

Fighting Blindness has established research programmes in many different aspects of eye research including a retinal microchip implant project in the National Microelectronics Research Centre in Cork. Its projects are at the cutting edge of international research and the Society is confident and determined to play a significant part in the international research effort to find treatments for all forms of blindness, especially retinal blindness which was its first area of interest.

In helping Fighting Blindness, the musicians who have already put Ireland on the international map through their own work are not only supporting attempts to find treatments for those who are suffering from the loss of their sight but they are also once again helping to raise Ireland's profile by supporting the outstanding work of Fighting Blindness in contributing to the international research effort to find treatments.

Michael Griffith
Chief Executive
Fighting Blindness
28th March, 2003

PHOTO CREDITS

Andrew Strong	The Irish Times
Brendan Bowyer	Des Lacey / Connie Lynch
Dervish	Pic 1 Christoph Obrecht
Damien Rice	Robbie Fry
David Agnew	Com Henry / Celtic Collections
David Holmes	D.Santini
Eleanor Shanley	The Irish Times
Gavin Friday	The Irish Times
Glen Hansard / The Frames	Zoran Orlic
Christy Moore	Sony Music
The Hot House Flowers	Patti Monaghen
Jack L	Declan English
Frances Black	Conor Horgan / Brian Allen
Westlife	BMG
James Galway	Hanya Chlala
The Corrs	Jason Bell
Luan Parle	Anne Holland
Mick Hanly	Anthony Hobbs
Neil Hannon	Hamish Brown
Relish	EMI / Tom Sheehan
Daniel O'Donnell	Rosette Records
Dominic Kirwin	Rosette Records
Pierce Turner	Tom Le Goff
The Saw Doctors	The Irish Times

All other images provided are used with kind permission by respective
Artist, Management and or Record Company.

To Hannah Swan

Sea de beathasa, Han

Contents

FOREWORD

GAY BYRNE

Over the years through my various radio and television programmes I have had the great honour of meeting and listening to many of the inspirational acts featured in this book. Indeed, I know that many of them were first exposed to the broad Irish public through their debut appearance on *The Late Late Show*. So it has understandably filled me with enormous pride to see their talents receiving subsequent acclaim.

From The Cradle to the Stage shows how ordinary Irish people from every part of the country have followed their dreams and in turn have given so much pleasure to millions of people at home and worldwide. From generation to generation, era to era and genre to genre, talented Irish singers, musicians and songwriters continue to surprise, entertain, inspire us and make us proud. From the swinging showband era of the sixties to our Grammy winners of later decades, from balmy summer days in Slane to intimate sessions in back rooms across the country, Irish music and Irish artists have carved out a special place in our hearts. And now through this book they are generously helping to ensure that much-needed funds are raised for the charity, Fighting Blindness.

As an avid reader myself, I have treasured the blessing of

having good sight throughout my life, and I firmly believe that most fully-sighted people cannot even begin to imagine the effect that blindness can have on a person's life. Sight is a boon we so often take for granted and we may tend to forget those who on a daily basis are denied the everyday joys of reading, watching television or films, experiencing the visual pleasures of nature or enjoying the simple delight of watching children and grandchildren growing up.

Throughout its 20-year history, Fighting Blindness has brought comfort to the many thousands of people who are progressively losing their sight through Retinal Degenerative Diseases. By buying this book you have helped fund their invaluable and crucial research into the development of treatments, and it is hoped that this progressive research will lead to future cures for these retinal diseases.

In the meantime, I hope you enjoy *From The Cradle to the Stage* as much as I have done. It will no doubt inspire many to translate their dreams into reality. But, most importantly, I hope that reading it helps to remind readers how blessed most of us are to have the fullness of our sight and to encourage us to offer a helping hand to those who don't.

1

ALTAN
Mairéad Ní Mhaonaigh, lead singer, violinist

No Irish traditional band has had a more significant impact on audiences and music lovers throughout the world over the past two decades than Altan, and their acclaimed singer and violinist Mairéad Ní Mhaonaigh has played a substantial role in that success. Altan's heartwarming, dynamic live performances have moved audiences from Donegal to Dublin, Tokyo to Seattle. Like their exquisitely produced award-winning recordings, an Altan concert can offer the most sensitive and touching old Irish songs alongside robust reels and jigs. Perhaps the *Chicago Weekly* best summed up the essence of the band when it wrote: "Thought by many to be the finest traditional Irish combo working today, Altan seamlessly blend dazzling instrumental prowess and the gorgeously delicate vocals of Mairéad Ní Mhaonaigh."

"My father played the fiddle when I was growing up. He did it very rarely then, because the music wasn't as popular as it is nowadays. He would take out the fiddle once in a while and start trying to go over the tunes he knew. I thought it was magical then. He would play nursery rhymes just to keep us amused. We thought he was fantastic altogether. Myself and my brother used to try and sit into the fiddle case while he was playing the fiddle. It's lovely to have memories that are so vivid so many years later. Of course I didn't realise then that I would end up playing the violin in later years. The fiddle is such a lovely-looking instrument. The very look of it was very appealing to me back then, but it was the sound of it that really enchanted me as a young child, because, as has been said, the sound of a fiddle is the nearest thing to the sound of a human voice.

My mother and father were big influences on my life. My mother is a very influential person for me because she more or less encouraged me to sing and to play music. My father encouraged me as well, but there was something more determined with my mother. She would say to me, "You should sing. If you have a voice, you should use it." But she was very shy about singing and expressing herself, so I think maybe I ended up doing the things she had really wanted to do. Perhaps she herself had not been encouraged as much as she should have been when she was young. My mother loved the idea of the human voice, not for the way it can be used to entertain as such, but simply for the sheer pleasure of being able to sing. Although she can play an instrument she's that little bit shyer about coming out with it, and maybe I aspired to realise her dreams. It's nice also when someone else has aspirations for you and you live up to them or near to them.

The first gig I ever went to would have been in Donegal where I come from. We went to a local hall where there were people playing music and dancing and singing traditional songs and I really loved it. There was such great appreciation for the music that I wanted to be up there myself, even though I wasn't able to sing or play at the time. That experience was a huge influence on my eventually becoming a singer and a musician.

On the other hand, making a career out of it just happened by accident. I wanted to become an artist at one stage. But to be practical I decided I should get myself a third level qualification, and after a number of years of study in Dublin I was conferred a Bachelor of Education.

But then when I was teaching for a while I realised that maybe it wasn't really what I wanted to do for a long-term career after all. There were people offering me opportunities for myself and my late husband Frankie Kennedy to record an album. That opened the door to lots of avenues and ideas, and we started to travel a little after we made that album and we noticed that we were enjoying the travelling and the playing. Both of us being educationalists we learned as much within one year of travelling than we had from all the books. Being naturally curious, and just loving the idea of going to different countries with our music, we bit the bullet and decided to take a career break from teaching and I've never looked back.

The important thing about music for me is that it's a very expressive activity. Music always lifts me and it goes way beyond just being happy or sad. It says things that go deeper than words, and I think it might have even saved me when Frankie died. I don't mean that in a high-fallutin' way, but it seemed to provide me with that little escape route whenever I needed it. Or maybe it offers you that little oasis of silence that you need and that you can find within music. That might seem contradictory, the idea of silence in music, but it gives you a sort of meditative way of healing yourself. What I didn't know was that people can pick up on what is happening to you through your music. For a long while I didn't realise how lucky I was that I had a way of trying to cope with such a loss as well as the usual ways of grieving, like crying and so on.

Music actually allowed me to stand back and observe myself from another perspective. It let me see how lucky I was that we had had such a good time when we'd been together. It helped me accept that he had been suffering and it was easier to let go after realising that he wasn't going to get better."

FAVOURITE SINGER/VOICE:
At the moment it's Joni Mitchell.

FAVOURITE ALBUM:
Blue by Joni Mitchell. I also like Norah Jones' album, *Come Away With Me*.

2

ANDREW STRONG

Born in Dublin, Andrew Strong first shot to national prominence in 1991 as the arrogant lead singer Deco Cuffe in *The Commitments*, Alan Parker's internationally successful film following the fortunes of a fledgling working-class Dublin soul band. The son of the legendary Irish singer Rob Strong who carved a reputation as a dynamic soul singer with the Irish showband The Plattermen, Andrew has subsequently enjoyed much success as a solo artist, especially in Scandinavia where his albums have sold phenomenally well. His debut album, *Out of Time*, earned him the accolade of being described as "the best living white man who sings soul music" by the *Observer Media Intelligence* in Denmark.

" My first vivid memory of music would have been from my dad Rob in an old pub called The Meeting Place on the north side of inner Dublin. While he was playing, I used to pick up bar glasses and customers would give me tips. That was probably my first real encounter with music. I can also remember that I used to stand at the side of the stage and play with my imaginary guitar. Obviously with my dad being in the business, seeing him perform live rubbed off on me a little, and so it was no surprise when I started to get my own bands together.

I had my first band in 1987 and we were called Perfect Stranger. We used to do covers of Joe Cocker songs as well as material we got from rock bands like Free, Bad Company and so on. I was actually in two bands at the same time, the second band using original material. I had got really into it at an early age and when I discovered music everything else just went out the window, including school studies. Luckily I got a part in *The Commitments* and it really took off from there.

As I grew up I never wanted to be anything other than a performer. But I'm a big fan of architecture and maybe I would have liked to have been an architect or followed some career like that, but the music bug caught me early. When I travel around a lot, as you do especially in the music business, I get great opportunities to appreciate the architecture of many cities and towns, like, for example, Copenhagen, where the architecture strikes me as very impressive. It's the same in Moscow which has buildings that seem to go on for days and days. That kind of stuff fascinates me.

The first show I can remember as a performer, was as a supporting act for my dad. Having Dad in the business ahead of me was a great help and encouragement. You could go "Right, Dad, you're playing here on Friday and you're playing there on Saturday and we're going to support you". My old man, being as easy-going as he is, would simply go "All right, yeah, no problem", and that was two more gigs for us!

In terms of influences and as far as support for my music goes, my folks have been a great help to me. When I look at what my dad has gone through in his career, and when I look at my career there are obviously things that are different. Times have changed since when he was first involved. Artists are a lot smarter these days, and they've learned how to protect themselves a lot more. So my parents have been very much involved and curious about my career as it progresses, especially my father who really respects what I do and admires me for having chosen the same profession as he did. He likes my records, and with every recording I make I finally realise it's okay when he says; "Yeah, you did a good job there".

The first couple of records I bought were by Kool and the Gang and Madness. That might not be very inspiring, but they were great bands, great for their time. But what really inspired me was simply the music itself. That there are no limitations to music and you are constantly having to reinvent yourself are some of the factors that have inspired me to stay in this business and, as they say, to 'take the bulls by the horns'.

As musical influences go I am a fan of a very diverse range of musical styles and performers. People who have inspired me when I was younger include Joe Cocker. I also loved the Beatles and Led Zeppelin, Jimi Hendrix and so on. Yes, you could say I'm a bit of a rocker as well as a soul singer."

FAVOURITE ALBUM: I could be predictable and name the Rolling Stones' *Exile on Main Street* or a Beatles album. Those were, and still are, fantastic records. But if I was stuck on a desert island with only one contemporary album it would have to be the new Audioslave album. Chris Cornell is such a great inspiration and a fabulous singer. If I were pushed to go for a golden oldie it would have to be The Beatles' *Sergeant Pepper's Lonely Hearts' Club Band*, or the Beach Boys' *Pet Sounds* or Rod Stewart's *Atlantic Crossing*.

3

ASH
Tim Wheeler, lead singer

Born in County Down, Tim Wheeler is the lead singer with Northern rock heroes Ash. An Ivor Novello Award winner for his songwriting ability, Tim Wheeler and Ash have enjoyed worldwide success with five top-selling albums to their name to date. Their list of hit singles includes 'Girl From Mars', 'Petrol', 'Uncle Pat', 'Oh Yeah', the infectious 'Shining Light' and the rifftastic 'Burn Baby Burn'. Their inventive work has featured in several Hollywood films, while the band continues to entertain live audience across the world with their energetic performances.

"Thinking back on my earliest memory of music, there was a lot of singing in school and in church. Mind you, my dad was probably the biggest influence on me because he wrote my very own song for me when I was a baby. It was called 'Little Black Bird' and was about a bird and a little boy called Timothy. Anytime I tell anyone this they just go "awww . . . how cute!" to wind me up.

There was always music in my family, my granny having won a gold medal for singing at the Dublin *Feis* way back around 1917. She was very musical. My dad has always played the piano. He's self-taught and never bothers reading music because he's got such a good ear for picking up the songs he hears. I remember hearing him play in the evenings while I was a kid drifting off to sleep. His music was very soothing. My big brother is also quite a singer. So I suppose I was force-fed music from an early age. But don't get me wrong - I'm not complaining!

As I got a little bit older, and was getting into pop music, I used to be glued to the radio and taped loads of songs off it. The first gig I ever went to was pretty uncool. It was Bon Jovi at the King's Hall in Belfast for my twelfth birthday present. The first concert I performed at was in school aged thirteen. Me and Mark from Ash started our first band when we were twelve. The band was called Vietnam and we were Iron Maiden wannabes. We somehow managed to persuade our headmaster to allow us to have a charity concert in aid of Comic Relief during a lunch break. In reality we were known as one of the worst bands in County Down, but of course we convinced each other we were great!

I had all sorts of dream professions in my head as a kid . . . I was going to be Tarzan, James Bond, Luke Skywalker, TJ Hooker and Indiana Jones. But as soon I got my first guitar, becoming a rock star was the only path that would do for me to follow, much to my mum's distress.

In 1992 myself and Mark Hamilton from Vietnam found drummer Rick McMurray, and by picking the first short word we liked in a dictionary, Ash was born. We funded our first demo with money we saved by starving ourselves during lunch break.

I have been very lucky. I have enjoyed so many terrific

moments in music with Ash, such as having a number one album at the age of nineteen. But one of the best was playing the Good Friday Agreement Referendum concert with U2 in Belfast, the gig during which John Hume and David Trimble joined hands on stage. That was a very emotional concert.

At the opposite end of things there have been times when I have felt frustrated, especially when we first experienced all the business side of the music thing. It was very disenchanting, but I've learned to accept it as a necessary evil and I just get on with it now. We work very hard when we're on tour and do all the promotional stuff, but when I get home, or I am in the studio, I make sure I can concentrate on the creative side. I firmly believe that you just have to keep the business and creative parts separate."

FAVOURITE SONG:
One of my favourite songs of all time is 'God Only Knows' by the Beach Boys. It's a very complex song when you examine it, yet it sounds very simple. It's a truly sublime work of genius.

FAVOURITE ALBUM:
Maybe I'd have to pick *Nevermind* by Nirvana. It changed my life when I was fifteen. It's very powerful, but it's also a pop record at heart and it contains so many great songs. In fact there isn't a bad song on it.

FAVOURITE ARTISTS:
Quite a few . . . Rolling Stones, Nirvana, Bob Dylan, Thin Lizzy, David Bowie, Jane's Addiction, Van Morrison, The Pixies, The Beatles, David Kitt, Sly and The Family Stone, Primal Scream, the Beach Boys, Weezer, The Undertones, the list could go on, and on, and on!

4

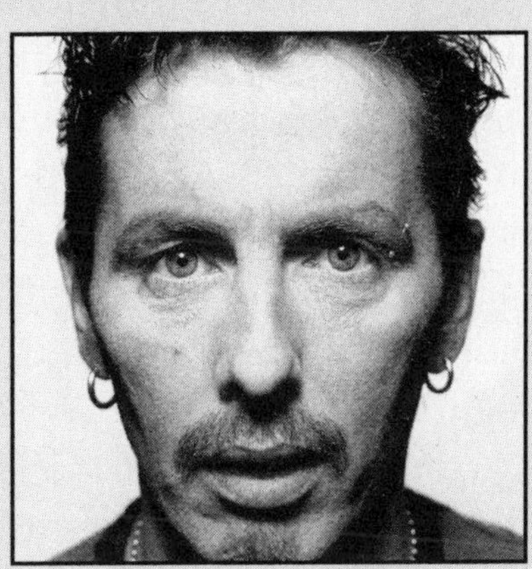

ASLAN
Christy Dignam,
lead singer

Christy Dignam is the lead singer with the long-established Dublin band Aslan. Aslan, which is also a Turkish word for 'lion', took their name from the heroic animal in C.S. Lewis' series of books chronicling the fictional land of Narnia. Formed in 1982, the band released their debut album, *Feel No Shame*, in 1987. Since then they have enjoyed enormous success with sell-out shows across Ireland and Europe. They have many platinum and gold albums to their name, have collected numerous awards, and wrote and recorded one of the most popular Irish singles of all time in 'Crazy World'.

When I was a very, very, very young kid I used to think that your ma and da were born a ma and da. And I remember this mate of mine on the street said to me, "Do you know that band Slade? Well they're from a place in England which is just like Finglas and they were all mates and they just got a band together and had lots of hits". That concept had never occurred to me until then, because I thought bands were born as fully-formed bands. I was probably only four or five at the time, but from that moment I said to myself, "Right, that's an excellent suss on the situation, and I could do that too". I've always loved singing, and all through my life, when I've been listening to songs like the Rolling Stones' 'Angie' I'd say to myself, "That song is going to be on my album when I'm a singer." Then when I was about fifteen I bought the album *The Times They Are A-Changin'* by Bob Dylan and from that moment I decided music could be a lot more then just a pop tune. That's when I decided 'This is it, man, I'm going to dedicate my life to music.'

But it was only when I got to the age of fourteen or fifteen that I realised that just because I *wanted* to be a singer it did not mean that I was automatically going to become one. I discovered that I had to work at it, otherwise it would never happen.

Not that it all happened straight away either. Over the years I've worked at a million jobs, including a spell on the Saint Patrick ferry from Rosslare to Le Havre. But through every job I ever had I felt inside that I was just biding my time before I'd make the move into music full-time. I never ever considered dedicating myself to doing anything else. All my life I've believed I was going to be a singer - end of story.

Then I got a job in Telecom Éireann as a telephone technician which at that time was a really secure, pensionable job. Me oul' man flipped when I told him I was jacking in the job to go full-time with the band. "Ya can't do that. That's a job for life!", he told me." You know the way das are! But I made the break and I've never ever thought of doing anything else since.

The biggest influence in my life (and I know that this will sound a bit sad to some people!) is my wife. I grew up with her and I've been with her since I was about thirteen years of age. She was always one hundred per cent behind me. I grew up in a place in Finglas on the north side of Dublin where everybody kept telling me "Will you snap out of it? You're not going to be a singer. You're only a knacker from Finglas", and that kind of thing. But my wife helped me to retain my belief in myself. She also supported me at the beginning when the band wasn't paying its way.

It's only the absolute love of what you do that keeps you going. I remember doing an interview with Shay Healy for RTE and he was saying "With all the knock-backs the band has suffered, blah blah blah, how did the band keep going?". But when you are doing something that you love so much then it doesn't feel like work. But perhaps if I had known at the beginning of this journey that it was going to be as hard as it turned out to be, then maybe I wouldn't actually have done it. Who knows?

The definitive moment when I knew this job would be the love of my life was when we were playing on the same bill as David Bowie at Slane. He's my hero, and my main musical influence. We were doing this song called 'The Sands Of Time' off the *Charlie Moonhead* album. During a part of the song where there's a long drum roll and a count of 1-2-3-4 into a big part, I looked across at the side of the stage where I saw Peter Frampton, who had big hits in the seventies, and Carlos Alomar, an incredible guitar player. When we did the drum roll bit they looked at each other and did high fives. To see two people who were my heroes, obviously admiring our music, little things like that mean so much. You can have a million people telling you that you are an eejit, but when people you admire tell you that you are doing the right thing, that's what keeps you going. It's what the people that matter to you say that really counts."

MAIN INFLUENCES: My main influences musically include David Bowie, Bob Dylan, Pink Floyd, Lou Reed and, of course, The Rolling Stones. I still think The Rolling Stones are the best rock'n'roll band ever.

FAVOURITE SONG: 'Letter from a Hooker in Minneapolis' from the album *Blue Valentine* by Tom Waits. Also 'Don't Give Up' by Peter Gabriel and Kate Bush.

FAVOURITE ALBUM: *The Rise And Fall Of Ziggy Stardust and The Spiders From Mars* by David Bowie. Also *Desire* by Bob Dylan.

5

BELLEFIRE

Bellefire are a three-piece band consisting of sisters Cathy and Ciara Newell from Galway and Sligo-born Kelly Kilfeather. They were formed after the legendary Louis Walsh auditioned thousands of young hopefuls for a new pop band back in 1999. In early 2001 they were invited to support Westlife, Destiny's Child and Boyzone for sell-out live concerts, while their debut Irish single 'Perfect Bliss' went straight into the charts at number 2! Since then they have enjoyed considerable success at home and abroad, including a number 1 hit in Japan, and have consolidated their status at home with a classy chart-busting interpretation of the U2 song 'All I Want Is You'.

CATHY NEWELL

"My mum and dad loved music, and I grew up surrounded by it. My earliest childhood memories of music are of being in the car when I was two or three. Dad would be driving, mum sitting up the front singing nursery rhymes and me trying to sing along in the back! I started playing classical violin at four and then started to play traditional as well. Myself and my sister Ciara went to an all-Irish school and used to be around ceili bands and learned *sean-nós* songs. I didn't really get into pop music until I was around seven or eight. My dad bought me my first album, by Kylie Minogue, and I got into the whole pop thing, singing in front of the mirror, dressing up in mum's clothes, putting on make-up and so on. I didn't know anybody who was a pop star. It's a dream when you're younger, but when you have to think of exams and serious stuff you forget the other life that's out there. But then the opportunity came along and now I'm actually doing what I've always dreamed about. One of my first idols was Kylie and she's as cool as ever, as are other artists who re-invented themselves over the years, like U2, Janet Jackson and Madonna. Meeting your heroes is the best feeling in the world. I met U2 at an awards ceremony. We were performing 'All I Want Is You' and looking down at the four lads in the audience giving it loads. It was the best feeling in the world! With the music business I take every day as it comes and I give it my best shot, but I don't dwell on things."

CIARA NEWELL

" My earliest memories would be the same as Cathy's. We played the violin and piano for five years and tried a lot of other instruments. Singing was just one thing we loved doing to pass the time. We were regularly asked up in front of family members and I used to love performing. We'd sing in the kitchen while Dad was cooking the dinner or Mum was ironing. I'd just sing away to myself. They had great patience with us!

Like Cathy, I was influenced by Kylie. We used to do 'the

locomotion' around the kitchen. I loved Whitney Houston and Celine Dion and as we got older we listened to everything in the charts. When I was at school my main goal was to be a singer, so I've wanted to do this all my life. I often wondered how to get into the business, so when I saw an advertisement about forming a band I went straight for it. I was just really, really lucky! It was hard when Bellefire first started. I was sixteen when I left home to join, although our parents were very supportive. It was a tricky decision, but their motto was - if we were happy, they were happy. The first show I ever went to, I was actually performing on stage and not in the audience! We were supporting Boyzone and I was backstage thinking "Ah, so this is what a concert is like!" It was weird, with all the bright lights, the glowing wands and the noise. The whole vibe was 'wow'. One of my best memories was doing *Top of the Pops*. I had watched it all my life and to be on it with Bellefire was part of my dream. I wouldn't change anything I've done with the band. We've travelled and sung in amazing places, made lots of fantastic fans and worked with really nice people. For the future I just want to be successful, get the albums out there and let the music do the talking."

KELLY KILFEATHER

❝ My memories of music go back really far. I was such a music fanatic from an early age. I remember as a toddler watching *Top Of The Pops* singing "Hands up, baby, hands up"! There are pictures of me in my nappy, hugging the television and crying when the programme was over. The first song I really got mad into was 'New Year's Day' by U2 when I was three. I used to be so happy whenever it came on the radio.

Television wasn't so important in our house and with a radio in every room I got a taste of every kind of music. My brothers and sisters were music fans too. One sister was into Chris de Burgh, so I didn't hang around her room too much! But my brothers were into all sorts, from David Bowie and Pink Floyd to The Flying Pickets. Hearing such a variety of styles kept me very open. Everyone in our family plays music and there were always instruments in the house to pick up. I lived, slept and drank music all day every day. But after the baby years I became very shy about singing, so it was a shock to the family when I joined Bellefire. My mother didn't hear me sing until I was on stage at The Point supporting Boyzone. She was more nervous for me then I was. My big influence was U2. The first album I bought was *The Joshua Tree*. The first gig I went to was U2. I was into the boy bands, but Pearl Jam were a favourite too. I like a good song and a good tune. Meeting your heroes is great too. When I met David Bowie I couldn't talk. He bought me a drink and I just sat there staring and going "I love you"! This is the best job in the world. I love what I do and I'm so glad I went for it because it has surpassed my expectations. I hope it lasts forever."

6

BRENDAN BOWYER
Royal Showband

Born in Waterford on October 12th 1938, Brendan Bowyer began his career with the Royal Showband in 1957. His dynamic singing style and energetic on-stage performances made him one of the most popular vocalists of the show-band golden days of the 1960s. Many hit records were chalked up along the way, none more memorable than the massively popular, and legendary, 'Hucklebuck', and the equally frantic 'I Ran All The Way Home'. In 1971 Bowyer left the Royal Showband and began performing in Las Vegas where he now lives, although he returns home to his beloved Ireland on a regular basis.

" My earliest musical memories are of my father, Stanley Bowyer, conducting operas in Limerick where I spent my early youth. I also remember being 'drafted' into the church choir at a very early age. It was the Redemptory Choir in Mount St Alphonsus (Boys and Men) and a great experience too.

In my youth the radio was as important to the people of Ireland as TV is now. I have cherished memories of the voice of Michael O'Hehir wafting through windows and doorways all over the city of Limerick on Sunday afternoons, not to mention the strains of the Artane Boys Band entertaining the crowds at Croke Park. The Radio Éireann programme, *Hospitals Requests*, was our main source of popular music until Radio Luxembourg made its mark in the fifties. The first big popular show I remember was called *Top Twenty*. It's wonderful to remember how we cherished these 'nuggets' of pop music compared with the media blitz we have today.

My parents met through music when my mother Maura went to my father, who was a professor of music, for vocal coaching in Waterford during the thirties. My mother sang opera, including a part in *Maritana* at the Olympia in Dublin, before marriage and children took over - it was a different world back then! Apart from being an operatic conductor my father was also highly accomplished at the violin and piano.

Thinking back over things that influenced me, the first gig I ever went to was at the Atlantic Ballroom in Tramore while I was still in school. It was during the mid fifties and the Clipper Carlton band were playing. I was entranced at their showmanship. Though I didn't realise it at the time, they were the forerunners of the big musical trend I was to be part of, where bands added an element of 'show' to the essential dance music for the eager patrons of the ballrooms.

Although I had fooled around in duos and trios for a while, the first real gig I did as a performer was with the Royal Showband at the Olympia Ballroom in Waterford back in September 1957. I never really thought of taking up any other profession after that. At that time, and still to this day, Waterford did not have a university college. My parents could not afford to send me to Dublin, Cork or Belfast for a medical, science (or whatever) degree. I sat for a bank exam, but luckily, as it happened, I didn't make the grade. However at that time I wasn't dreaming of a career in music. I thought it would be a wonderful thing to do, but not quite possible in the Ireland of the late fifties.

I have had some lovely memories in the music business, but it's difficult to pinpoint one exact memory above all; there have been so many peaks and valleys since 1957. Just recently I made an album for Universal Records called *Follow On*, a celebration of Irish singer/songwriters. Recording had been something I had neglected for a while, but I was especially pleased with its success. Most of the musicians on it were alumni of one of Van Morrison's great touring bands, people like Johnny Scott and Bobby Irwin. But I got a special thrill when *Hot Press* magazine made it 'Record of the Month' when reviewing it. Looking back further, however, the most significant moment for me was probably in 1961 when the Royal Showband were awarded the Carl Alan Award in Great Britain, for 'Best Modern Dance Band'. For dance bands playing in Britain it was akin to winning an Oscar. I probably should also mention the night that the Beatles played support to us. That was such a special musical moment I can still remember the date - April 14th 1962.

Despite the fact that I've brought many problems on myself through alcohol, including periods of neglect and apathy, I have really never lost my love of music and entertainment."

FAVOURITE SONG: Elvis Presley singing 'My First, My Last, My Everything'. Although I grew up in a family steeped in a classical music background, when I first heard Elvis singing 'Heartbreak Hotel', 'That's All Right, Mama', 'Hound Dog' and 'Don't Be Cruel' I was transformed. It was rock'n'roll for me after that. Other than the afore-mentioned songs, 'Smoke

Gets In Your Eyes' by the Platters is another very special favourite.

FAVOURITE ALBUM: I remember loving Van Morrison's *Tupelo Honey*. Van was a pioneer in his own right, and was in the Monarchs Showband in Belfast. He was one of many famous artists who have played support to the Royal Showband.

7

BRIAN KENNEDY

Brian Edward Patrick Kennedy is one of Ireland's most unique vocal stylists as well as one of our most successful musical ambassadors. One of six children born into the Kennedy clan, Brian was born on 12th October 1966 and brought up in the Falls Road in Belfast. He discovered his singing voice during music class at school when he found he could hear any note and then repeat it pitch perfect. He would also regularly harmonise with whatever song came on the radio. Since the release of his first album, *The Great War of Words*, in 1990, Brian Kennedy has repeatedly reaffirmed his remarkable and unique talent, and audiences all over the world continue to return to experience his superb live performances. He has had three albums in the Top 30 of the Irish album charts simultaneously. But he is not only a prolific songwriter but also a master interpreter too, and has been described by *Q* magazine as having "a voice to charm the angels".

" Music had a hard time getting to my ears on the Falls Road in Belfast, so when it did get through it was greeted with great enthusiasm. The local shop was situated in a house and had a washing line of vinyl albums pegged up on display. There was one by a group called The Flying Column with a song called 'Four Green Fields' written by the legendary Tommy Makem. I was fascinated by the man's voice and the fact that the album cover featured Ireland in the shape of an old woman with a spinning wheel. The melancholy stopped me in my tracks.

My parents didn't really have a musical background. They didn't really have the time, I suppose. But my mother would often sing the line "It's getting better" over and over while she worked away at the sink. I just assumed she was singing about our family situation. Years later I heard the rest of what I then discovered was a song by the Mamas and Papas. My pa was a big Al Jolson fan, especially when his films came on the television, and Perry Como was a favourite singer of both my parents. So our house was more of a TV house, and the radio wasn't such a big influence.

The first gig I ever went to was at Queen's University in Belfast. It was loud and very hot. Among the sea of leather jackets and perms I was the only one in a duffel coat. I was too scared to take it off in case I lost it, even though I was boiling with the heat. I remember one of the bouncers punched an over-eager fan off the stage and the lead singer in turn punched the bouncer and the crowd roared at them. I remember spotting the words 'Def Leppard' written on someone's jacket and wondering what it meant.

My music teacher at school (God love him!) was the first person who told me I could be a singer if I really wanted to. I think singing is something that chooses you rather than the other way round, and I don't remember consciously deciding to become a singer. But I was simply one of those annoying kids, constantly humming some tune or other and always thinking of harmonies, even for ambulance sirens!

The first wee gig I did myself was at the school disco with a band called Beyond The Melting Pot. We played covers, of course, and I can recall looking forward to singing the song 'Only You' which had been a big hit for Yazoo. I was terrified at the prospect, but I was also determined to make it work.

I've had so many influences on my musical career over the years. I've sung with Van Morrison, Bob Dylan, John Lee Hooker, Bonnie Raitt and Stevie Wonder. I've met Joni Mitchell, Kate Bush and Jeff Buckley and been lucky enough to sing on Broadway.

Of course there have been some frustrating times too. After I left RCA Records the first time, I cut off my hair and took a train around America. I was seriously deflated by the split, but after a month or so of travelling and spontaneous singing I reminded myself why I was doing it in the first place. I realised that without artists there wouldn't be an industry, rather that the other way around. Then Van Morrison got in touch and everything changed."

FAVOURITE SONG: 'A Case of You' by Joni Mitchell.

FAVOURITE ARTIST: I love all sorts of people. My tastes are very varied and include Joni Mitchell, Aretha Franklin, Kate Bush, Tom Waits, Stevie Wonder, Nat King Cole, Tony Bennett, Sam Cooke, Van Morrison, Eddi Reader, Kirsty McColl, Cocteau Twins, Bonnie Raitt, Prince, Mary Coughlan, Dolores Keane, Paul Brady, U2, Billie Holiday, Ella Fitzgerald.
Artists either move me or they don't. I'm either convinced by the singer or I'm not. I believe all the people above convince me, and more.

8

BRÍDÍN BRENNAN

Coming from one of the most remote and picturesque parts of Ireland (Gweedore in County Donegal), Brídín is the youngest of the musically famous Brennan family. Her well known siblings include Enya, and Moya from Clannad. When she was eighteen she was invited to perform backing vocals on the Clannad album, *Anam*, and shortly afterwards joined them for a world tour. This became the pattern over Clannad's next two albums, and besides touring she also got to appear on many of the world's top television shows including *Tonight With Jay Leno*. She then decided to take some time off from music to decide her future. In London she experienced a varied selection of music, and was invited by a friend to perform lead vocal tracks on his album. It being a different style of music, it rekindled her desire to sing and she began to write her own music for the first time. She then linked up with a production team in Dublin. One of the first tracks she recorded was released to radio in Ireland, became a Top 30 Hit and generated intense media interest in her. She is currently finishing material for her debut album.

❝I remember entering choir competitions when I was at school and being so excited learning my own harmony parts over and over. I was always interested in singing harmony. Even today when I hear a song on the radio I listen out for the harmony. When our school choir won the Ulster final it was very exciting.

I used to watch my older brothers and sisters singing and wanted to do what they were doing. I used to sing in the church choir, the school choir and on my father's stage in Leo's Tavern.

The radio was always a big influence on me. My parents used to listen to Radio na Gaeltachta all the time, so that brought the traditional influence. Then when I grew older I listened to pop music radio. The next day at school we would discuss all the songs we had listened to the night before. From then on it was a healthy mix of the traditional and the pop influences.

My parents were also a huge influence in other ways. My mother used to teach music at our local secondary school, Pobail Scoil Ghaoth Dobhair. She taught keyboards to kids aged six to twelve, and was the musical director at our local theatre. Although she's now retired, she still plays organ and is the head of the church choir.

My father Leo was in a band called the Slieve Foy Dance Band with other members of his family. They used to play shows around Ireland, England and Scotland. He opened a pub at home called Leo's Tavern in the late sixties or thereabouts. He still entertains, but my brother Bartley now runs it.

There was always music going on in our house. If it wasn't traditional it was classical, jazz, rock and roll, or pop. When Clannad (who consisted of my two brothers, my sister and two uncles) used to go on tour in the early days they would arrive home with the likes of Donal Lunny, Paul Brady, Christy

Moore, Ronnie Drew or some other fantastic performer, and they would go down to Leo's Tavern for a jam session.

The first gig I ever went to, apart from the gigs at home, must have been U2. I was quite young and didn't know what to expect, but, boy, was I blown away! Even now after seeing them a few times I still get blown away. Thinking back to the first proper gig I ever sang at, it was as backing vocalist with Clannad. I was so nervous I think I made everybody else nervous. But I remember walking off stage afterwards and thinking "Wow, that felt good!"

Despite coming from such a musical family, I never seriously thought that music would become a full-time career for me. At school I was looking at every other possible career because I thought there were enough members of the family already playing music. So at first I thought I'd be an air-hostess. But I wasn't tall enough, and I didn't think I'd really have the guts to be brave if anything went wrong. Then I thought hair-dressing might be the right career for me, but after thinking about it for over two years, I knew I wasn't cut out for it either.

Then I joined Clannad for a few years as a backing vocalist. I still wasn't quite sure if that was the road I wanted to take, so I moved to London where I still live. I worked at various jobs - as a receptionist, in catering, and even as a food safety advisor. But I realised I missed the music, so I went back into it. I started to write my own material and became more interested in being the main vocalist rather than backing vocalist.

So it's taken me a while to get to where I am today. There have been some frustrating moments along the way. It's almost five years since I started writing the material for my current album, which will be released soon. Delay like that can be frustrating. One minute a record company will tell you they are really interested in you. The next minute they're not. I think that some record companies are more interested in boy/girl bands and releasing cover versions while there are so many great artists out there who are writing their own material. Hopefully that will change soon.

I have had some great moments in music so far, but the best has to have been when I released my first single in Ireland. It was called 'Hang On'. I couldn't get over the amount of airplay it got. It was something I had written myself and there it was being played on the radio! I'd get so excited every time I'd hear it."

FAVOURITE SONG: It's such a hard question, because one week I could be listening to David Gray and then I'd change to the Red Hot Chili Peppers or Daniel Beddingfield or U2. It depends on my mood, or whom I want to be influenced by that week.

FAVOURITE SONG: 'A Little Less Conversation' by Elvis Presley

FAVOURITE ARTIST: Alanis Morissette - she really knows how to perform.

FAVOURITE ALBUM: *Off the Wall* by Michael Jackson. Maybe he's a little off the wall himself today, but he wrote some cracking songs.

9

CARA DILLON

Born in 1975 in Dungiven, Co. Derry, Cara Dillon is considered to be one of the hottest new talents in Irish music. At the early age of fourteen she won the coveted All-Ireland Singing Trophy. Over the years since then she has worked with artists of the calibre of Phil Coulter and Mike Oldfield. In 1995 she joined the group Equation but left a year later to pursue a solo career. In 2002 she was voted Best Newcomer in the BBC Folk Awards, while *Hot Press* magazine acclaimed her as Best Roots Act that same year. Her self-titled debut album was released to widespread critical acclaim, followed by her much-anticipated second album, *Sweet Liberty*, in 2003. Cara Dillon's unique singing voice promises to deliver a hugely successful future for her at home and abroad.

" Some of my fondest memories are of the many fleadhs that were held every year in my hometown of Dungiven. It was a great town to grow up in; there was always music on the streets every summer. Lots of musicians and singers from all over the country would gather there. We would have workshops in the local school and it's there I learned how to play the fiddle and the bodhran. Everybody was handed a tin whistle or a fiddle at some point. It was a great place.

My sister Mary used to sing in a band. She is ten years older than I and really encouraged me to take a big interest in singing. There were lots of traditional singers in the family, all well known in the area. So, there was really no way of escaping music. Besides, you would have all your teachers telling you about your local history and all the legendary songs that related to it. There was definitely no way of avoiding it!

I enjoyed music so much. Ireland is so full of history and the traditions of music, song and dance are so powerful. There's a song called 'The Gem of the Roe' which is featured on my album, *Sweet Liberty*. It was one of the first songs I ever learned, when I was about eight or nine. It has a melody so simple and beautiful, and it tells a story about a princess who grew up in a castle in a town. I grew up listening to stories from my parents about their uncles emigrating, leaving home for the first time, and what it was like in the house before they left. They were very, very haunting tales. Over the years I've learned songs about emigration, so it's like a big puzzle that has come together. I can relate to what the songs are about because they connect with what actually happened to my own family.

I realised that music could be a career for me when I was in a folk band called Óige with my two best friends. I was about fifteen and we played during our secondary school years to earn a bit of pocket money. We did really well to the point that we travelled to Israel and throughout Europe playing at festivals. That really gave me a taste of what it would be like to do it professionally. I then joined a band called Equation and we were offered a deal by Warners, the major record company.

I was eighteen at the time. I had a choice either go to university or go with this opportunity which would allow me to do what I loved doing. So I went down the singing route and I haven't looked back since.

I've kind of always known that this is what I wanted to do, although for a while I thought I wouldn't mind doing a bit of teaching. I was never very sure about teaching, but I thought it might be something that I could do while I'd continue with my passion for singing. Teaching would be my side job! Through all the times when there was career planning at school and when everyone was wondering what they were going to do to earn a living, most of that time I spent in the corner with my two friends saying "Right, we've got an hour now which is supposed to be career planning, so let's figure out what to take with us to Germany for our two months' tour!"

My total love of the music keeps me going. I had that record deal with Warners for five or six years up until two years ago. There were a lot of down points as well as the highs you get when signed to a major record label. There have been times when I felt like quitting and doing something 'normal'. But every time I got to that point I'd sit back and think "This is my complete passion. This is what I absolutely love doing and I'm going to stick at it".

I'm very, very happy at what I do. Music is such a wonderful thing to be involved in. There's so much to learn and so many new people to meet. We are constantly meeting songwriters and musicians at festivals and hooking up and working with them. Recently I met a man who came to one of our gigs and he gave me his phone number and address. He has since passed on a wealth of songs that I hadn't discovered before. I'm very excited about going through these songs.

One of the highlights of the past couple of years for me was going to the *Hot Press* awards. One minute I was a traditional folk singer working away on my own thing and then all of a sudden I'm getting an award at one of the most prestigious Irish music events of the year. It was great to be sitting in a room with U2 and The Corrs and the other top acts. It was really fantastic to meet these people, and everybody respecting each other for what they do musically.

The old image of Irish traditional musicians in Aran jumpers has completely gone out the window and everybody thinks it's so cool nowadays, which is wonderful. It's always been brilliant, but it's just now that people are finally opening up to it. People are being more open-minded and I'm so proud to be part of it."

FAVOURITE SONG: Kate Bush 'The Hound of Love'

FAVOURITE ALBUM: as above

FAVOURITE SINGER: Kate Bush

BIGGEST INFLUENCE: W B Yeats, for his poetry and his love of the land. Sometimes I read his poetry to get inspiration for melodies.

10

CARLY HENNESSY

Born in Dublin, Carly Hennessy has enjoyed significant success with her international debut album, *Ultimate High*. Having developed a keen ear for music at just nine years of age, she beat 2,000 other hopefuls for the role of Little Cosette in the international production of the musical, *Les Miserables*. A year later she recorded her debut album, a collection of holiday favourites entitled *Carly's Christmas Album*, which was distributed across Ireland and the UK only. Subsequently signed to US record giant MCA Records at the age of fifteen, Carly has had the opportunity of collaborating and working with some the leading songwriters in the music world. In 2003 she won Best Irish Female at the Meteor Irish Music Awards, an achievement that had the added significance of having been decided by the votes of the discerning Irish music public.

❝My earliest memory of music would have to be listening to Madonna around the house. There was always music in the house. My family would regularly have sessions at home, and friends would come over to play music for hours. There would be such a variety of music styles, from Fleetwood Mac to The Pretenders. Even though I was quite young at the time I never knew who New Kids on the Block were! I thought it was normal for a four or five year old to be listening to Neil Young and The Eagles. Another early memory of music in my life goes back to Diana Ross. I learned all the words of her hits and I would do the little routines she did in her videos over and over again. My whole life was surrounded by music. Between my brother recording in his bedroom and the random sessions, it was everywhere. I remember my brother recording on his little Dictaphone machine. He would be half way through recording a song, trying to get it perfect, until I walked into the room to ask for something and ruin his recording efforts! I was always something of an entertainer and one of those kids who had loads of energy. In fact I had so much of it that my mother decided to focus it into one thing and music was something that she realised distracted me. So with her encouragement I would be up on the kitchen table performing as often as I could.

The first gig I ever went to, believe it or not, was either Kylie Minogue or Jason Donovan. I can't remember which of them it was because I was so young at the time. But I was big into Kylie when I was growing up. This was unusual because I wasn't that keen on listening to the radio. I was happier listening to records, and I listened to a lot of theatre stuff, like the musical, *Annie*. I used to get musicals on tape and would listen to them so often that I got to know every single word. So when it came to auditioning for the part of Annie in a production that was coming up, I didn't have to learn any of the words because I'd known them off perfectly since I was about four.

I never ever thought that I would be anything else other than a performer. From the time I was a kid I've always wanted to be famous. It never crossed my mind even once that there might be something else I could do with my life. I always knew I was going to do what I'm doing now. I was good at school, but I knew that the music business had something in store for me, so I made my first album when I was ten and it went on from there.

I'll go to the ends of the earth to make this happen. This is my life. I genuinely believe that everyone is born to achieve something specific and my niche in life is to be a singer and a performer. Whether I become hugely famous or not, I don't have any urge to do any other job. All my friends and all my family knew that this was going to be my job and I've always stuck to that.

My best moment in music so far was meeting Mick Jagger and thinking he was Steve Tyler from Aerosmith. He was really cool and a very nice guy. We spent about three days together in a studio in the USA. Supporting Brian Adams was also a huge event for me. But everything is a best moment in a way. Every day brings its own fresh learning experience. When I signed my record deal that was a great moment. Then it changed to when I recorded my album. But I have to say the whole thing has been just incredible, one amazing adventure."

FAVOURITE SONG: I actually have two, 'Seven Wonders' by Fleetwood Mac, and The Pretenders' 'Some Stay the Same'.

FAVOURITE ALBUM: *Thriller* by Michael Jackson.

FAVOURITE SINGER: Stevie Nicks.

11

CHRISTY MOORE

Christy Moore was born in May 1945 in Co Kildare. One of the most talented performers of his generation, his premier standing in Irish folk music is unrivalled and unquestioned. Christy first came to the attention of Irish audiences as a folk performer in the early 60s. While touring in England he recorded and released his first album before joining the legendary Planxty. His relationship with that band continued on and off throughout the 70s until he and Donal Lunny left to form the equally formidable Moving Hearts. But despite the success of the bands of which he has been such a vital member he has always shone brightest in the solo spotlight. His songs have become national treasures, from his own 'Lisdoonvarna' to his interpretation of Jimmy MacCarthy's 'Ride On'. Alongside countless music awards, much critical acclaim and numerous multi-platinum selling albums, Christy Moore has also enjoyed the achievement of a best-selling book, titled *One Voice*.

"Hearing my mother sing, both in the home and in the Dominican Church on Sundays, would be one my earliest memories of music. She played the piano and sang a lot. She was a beautiful singer. When you're a child you tend not to notice these things. It doesn't strike you. It's just another thing going on in the house and you just take it as normal. It's only many years later that you realise that not everybody has a mother who sings all the time, or as beautifully.

I really started to enjoy singing as soon as I began singing in choirs, like the choir in the Patrician Brothers' national school in Newbridge run by a Brother Michael. It was the first realisation I had that I really enjoyed singing. There was also a woman called Mrs Sullivan who had a school of music in Newbridge that I used to attend. She used to put on concerts too. So at a very early age I became aware of voices and the power of voices and the beauty of harmony and the kind of feeling you get when a number of voices sing together in harmony. When you're part of it it's an amazing feeling.

In my younger days there were different things I wanted to be, but it didn't dawn on me that I'd like to be a singer until I was sixteen or seventeen. That's when I thought, "Jesus I'd love to do that!" I saw the Clancy Brothers and Tommy Makem singing in Dublin in 1961 and shortly after that I saw Liam Clancy in Bunclody standing on the street, playing the guitar and singing, and I was just awestruck by the wonder of it all. To see and hear this man singing such great songs, it was a huge turn-on. What an effect it had on me; this man standing on a street with his head back, playing the guitar and singing these magical songs. It was the songs that really did it for me; I hadn't been exposed to the Clancy Brothers' repertoire growing up, but when I heard them I just thought they were fantastic. When I saw him then in the flesh on the street it was just like, "This is brilliant!" That definitely was a big turning point, although it would be another four or five years before I would do it myself.

The first song I ever wrote and completed was called 'Ninety Miles to Dublin Town'. An awful lot of the music thing today is about writing your own songs, but for the first ten years of my professional career it never even occurred to me to write my own songs. At the time I became a singer it was all about sourcing old material and it was all to do with finding old songs and presenting them in a new way. I was quite happy with all of that, and it only changed when I got to hear certain people who wrote songs, particularly Ewan McColl, the father of the late Kirsty McColl. He wrote great songs like 'The First Time Ever I Saw Your Face' and 'Dirty Old Town'. I heard him for the first time in 1967, but I wasn't to write a song for another ten years. I had ten albums recorded before I wrote a song. There was no need to write songs early on and I still do mainly other people's work. I'm not a very prolific writer myself. On my last two albums there might have been two or three of my own songs and that was all. I would prefer to sing a good song by another writer than a bad song written by myself. Sometimes I think there's too much emphasis on the whole area of writing. People are very hung up on "Did you write that yourself?" but I don't think it matters a shite. I like to sing songs, but I don't feel I have to write them all.

Another big influence on me was the radio. It was all radio when I was a young fella. The radio was the centre of the universe. When I was growing up in Newbridge I was fortunate in that I spent a lot of time with grandparents, my mother's people and my father's mother. I spent a lot of time in both their houses and the wireless was the big thing then. This was in the early 1950s when radio was really respected. It occupied a more sacred place than the television set occupies now. People had a respect for it and a real awe towards it.

People sat down and gathered round specifically to listen to certain programmes. In Dowlings, my grandmother's place, they had no electricity and the wireless was battery-powered. They used to have these big batteries and I can still remember listening to races and to particular music programmes. Even the Angelus had a vibe off it. Yes, radio played a huge part in my young life.

I don't think I have any single favourite memory of music. It's an on-going thing for me. In general, when I go out and sit down in front of an audience of people, I think it's such a privilege to be able to share a song. It's wonderful to communicate with people through the singing of a song and to feel that we all go into this place for three or four minutes together for as long as the song lasts. It's such a fantastic privilege to have this in my life. I never take it for granted and I am so thankful for it. To be given these gifts, to be able to hear a good song and learn a good song and sing a good song feels such a great privilege in my life."

FAVOURITE SONG:
If I was allowed to hear one song before I die I would love to hear my mother sing 'Ave Maria'.

12

THE
CORRS

Jim Corr

Born and raised in Dundalk, Jim Corr is the eldest member of the superstar musical family The Corrs that also includes his famous sisters Andrea, Caroline and Sharon. Regarded by many music business insiders as the hardest-working band in the music industry, The Corrs have amassed worldwide album sales in excess of 24 million. They are indeed a global phenomenon, merging an attractive physical image with what appears to be an effortless creativity that appeals to fans from as far apart as Ireland and Japan. Having earned platinum albums in more than twenty countries, The Corrs have become one of the most successful Irish pop exports of the past twenty years.

" My parents had a band which they played in on a semi-professional, local level. So my most vivid memories of music from when I was a child are of sitting listening to my dad playing the organ or the piano and listening to both my parents rehearsing. There were many aspects of their playing that made me pay close attention to what they did, and noticing the amount of fun they had with their music was one important factor that attracted to me to it. But I believe that when you grow up in a musical environment, where music is basically your parents' job, it rubs off on you. So all of us, Andrea, Caroline and Sharon included, were very much influenced by what we saw and heard them doing. It grabbed us and encouraged us towards careers in music.

As the eldest in the family I was the first one to have a job, so I could afford to buy albums, and the girls tended to listen to whatever I was listening to. There were regular fights to get to the piano and play it, so we often had to take it in turns for the sake of peace like any other family. But maybe unlike some families we didn't have different types of music coming out of different rooms in the house, simply because there was only one music system in the house for quite a while. So we weren't competing in terms of putting on different types of music, and we generally liked what each of us as individuals listened to anyway.

I really started considering going professionally into music when I was thirteen or so and when I got my first guitar. I had been playing piano for quite a few years before that. When I got that guitar and started having lessons on it from a neighbour the whole idea of being in a band started to really appeal to me. So myself and a couple of guys from Dundalk started our own band, and the first gig I ever played live was with them. We gigged on a local level for a couple of years, playing and writing our own music. It was great fun, and the love we had for what we were doing became deeply ingrained in all of us. There was a little fear as well, of course, and one of the lads often got physically sick with stage fright before a gig started. But sure that's normal and happens to the best musicians. All told, it was a very satisfying and fulfilling experience to be playing our own music and to have people come along, like it and support us. Those early positive experiences helped me make the decision to go fully professional.

One of the first bands I saw live (apart from my parents') would have been Catch 22 from the North of Ireland. They played in a local club in Dundalk and I used to go along and see them as often as I could. I was probably under the legal age for getting into the premises at the time, but they were a brilliant band and thinking of them now brings alive so many exciting memories of seeing music being performed live on stage for the first time.

Then came a pivotal point. After I had been working for some time with various bands and musicians and doing session work, I was offered an attractive job playing keyboards with a well-known artist. But at the back of my mind I had the thought that it would be a great idea to form The Corrs because it had become so obvious that my sisters were also very musical. So I put a lot of thought into it, decided to turn down the offer and went back home to Dundalk, where I rented a house, set up a wee studio and started writing and recording with my sisters. It wasn't long before we auditioned for *The Commitments*, the film based on Roddy Doyle's book.

Many people have encouraged me throughout my music career, apart from my parents. I love the Police and was heavily influenced by what they did. Other influences include Fleetwood Mac, The Beatles, Scritti Politti (whom I loved too), and The Beach Boys. We listened to such a wide variety of music in our house, including whatever our parents were listening to, so we were influenced by a very wide selection of artists in lots of different genres.

My best moment so far in music was going on stage in Lansdowne Road in Dublin to play before 55,000 people or some enormous number like that. The highlight was when the curtains went back and the crowd roared and cheered. That was truly wonderful! We've also had the chance to meet a lot of great people, like Nelson Mandela, the Pope, two American Presidents and lots of other impressive individuals. Of course, it's very pleasant to be able to do things like that. But you tend to forget a lot of stuff because it happens so fast. It's very much like a whirlwind as we travel from city to city, country to country, suffering from jetlag, trying to fit in all the gigs and the promotional duties. So you might not be as fully aware as to what's happening around you, as you'd like to be. But it's exciting when you think back and recall such memorable occasions like those I've mentioned. We'll all certainly have great stories for our grandchildren, that's for sure!"

FAVOURITE ALBUM:
Fleetwood Mac *Rumours*

FAVOURITE SONG:
'I Wanna Be With You Everywhere' by Fleetwood Mac.

13

THE CRANBERRIES

Fergal Lawler, drummer, percussionist

Fergal Patrick Lawler was born on 4th March 1971 in Limerick. Drummer, percussionist and a founding member of The Cranberries, Fergal has enjoyed considerable international acclaim with a band who are now accepted as one of Ireland's most dynamic musical exports. The Cranberries have enjoyed many international hit singles, including 'Zombie', 'Linger' and 'Ode To My Family'. Their debut album, *Everyone Else is Doing It, So Why Can't We?*, in March 1993 was a huge commercial success worldwide, and it set the band on the road to a level of international stardom that saw them score millions of album sales with works of the calibre of *'No Need To Argue'* and *'Wake Up And Smell The Coffee'*.

" My first memory of being moved by music goes back to when I was around three or four years of age. I remember sitting in my parents' rocking chair in my dad's music room, listening to 'Fernando' by Abba over and over

again. I'd like it to have been something more 'hip', like The Beatles or Pink Floyd, but I was only three or four!

Radio was one of the main instigators in the whole process of me getting into music. I listened to the radio religiously in my youth, illegally making compilations of my favourite songs, just like many an Irish youth did at the time. I was mostly interested in chart music until I hit my teens and discovered Dave Fanning and pirate radio.

Apart from the radio, my parents were another major factor in my musical growth, although nobody in the house played an instrument. My dad is a huge fan of opera and classical music and has been collecting records since he was fifteen years old. So I'm sure they were well impressed when I suggested getting a nice 'classical' instrument - a drumkit! But they agreed and were very encouraging and never complained about the noise.

The first gig I ever went to was U2 in Páirc uí Caoimh in Cork in 1987. I was around sixteen and I went with Noel, Mike and a load of other friends. UB40 were the support act on the bill and they were brilliant. I was blown away by the whole thing and ended up missing my train home because I insisted on staying right to the very end. My mates had all gone to catch the earlier train, so I was presumed to be 'missing in action'. Luckily there was a later train, so there was no need for them to have been so worried about me after all.

The first gig I ever played with The Cranberries was in a club called Ruby's in Limerick. We were the opening act for a local band called They Do It With Mirrors. It was 'Leaving Cert Results Night', so it was totally jammed. We had about six songs and we were all seriously nervous. I think I even puked a few times, but in the end it went well. It took all of us more than a year to get used to playing in front of people, whereas now it's more of an excited feeling I get instead of a nervous one.

To be honest, I didn't really have a clue what I wanted to do when I finished school. I began playing drums seriously about six months after I did my Leaving Cert, and it was one of the few things I felt confident doing. I suppose it was just destiny.

Anytime I'm asked to name my best moment in music it's always a very difficult question to answer. There hasn't really been one defining moment. In fact, the whole experience has been fantastic most of the time. On the other hand, there has been the occasional period when, because of the heavy work-load, I've felt frustrated and thought I'd had enough of the music business. For example, we had to cancel the tour planned to support our third album, *To The Faithful Departed*, as we hadn't taken a holiday since we had begun the band about five years previously. We were all completely burned out and disillusioned by everything. We took almost a year off and when we toured after our fourth album, *Bury The Hatchet*, we took it much easier, with a few weeks on and a few weeks off, and that way of operating has worked well for us since then."

FAVOURITE ARTIST
This is always the most difficult question to answer! There have been SO many favourite artists over the years, so the best I can do is to give you a list of some of them. The Beatles, The Clash, The Smiths, Led Zeppelin, Pink Floyd, The Cure, The Pixies, The House Of Love, The Cocteau Twins, U2, REM, Grant Lee Buffalo, Radiohead, Bob Marley, Jeff Buckley, Pearl Jam, Nirvana, Coldplay, Blur and many more I just can't think of right now. The reason I've loved all of these bands is more of a subconscious thing. They are the artists who move me the most. They give me a feeling that I get from nothing else.

14

DAMIEN DEMPSEY

Hailing from Donaghmede in North Dublin, 26-year singer-songwriter Damien Dempsey first came to the attention of Irish ears in 1997 with the track 'Dublin Town' of which Shane McGowan, among many illustrious others, sang its praises. "It's angry, but it's humorous, with great music and great lyrics. He's similar to me as a songwriter. He sees the beauty that is Ireland and that was Ireland's past and that can be Ireland's future," the Pogues man declared. Having collaborated with various artists, including U2 producer Brian Eno, and touring with stalwart musicians such as Christy Moore and Sinead O'Connor, Damien Dempsey looks set to enjoy further success with the 2003 release of his second album titled *Seize The Day*.

" Probably my earliest memory of music as a child is of simply sitting at home during a house party. My parents would arrive home from the pub, say at Christmas time, with all the aunties and uncles, and a music session would soon get under way. The oul' sing-a-long would grab my attention. There wouldn't be anyone playing instruments - they just sang, but I loved it. Apart from that sort of thing going on in the house every now and then, they would have been listening to The Dubliners and Christy Moore. In fact there would be all sorts of music in the house, from the folk and ballads to the 'ska' music my brothers would all be listening to. So I would hear records by Madness and the Specials, and Bob Marley was huge as far back as I can remember in working-class Dublin. I don't know if it was the same all around the country, but he was very big in Dublin through the eighties. Everyone was playing him. So all of that would have been soaking in. Ska, reggae and traditional stuff. I was soaking it all in like a sponge, as you do when you're a kid.

I think when Phil Lynott died in 1986 Dublin went into a state of mourning for him, and we dealt with our grief by playing his records all the time, all over Dublin. I remember my brother called me into the front room and he just said, "Listen to this." And the first notes of 'Whisky in the Jar' by Thin Lizzy rang out. The whole band blasted in and Philo's raw bassy voice really kicked. I was bitten at that moment and I think that was the moment, way back in the late eighties, when I decided I had to get myself a guitar. So I saved a few bob and my father helped me out too and I got myself a little banger of a yoke. From then on I spent as much time as I could teaching myself to play it. I saved up more money and a year later I bought an electric guitar and I started learning to play all the solos. I wasn't into singing at that stage, just into the playing and the solos and all the Thin Lizzy riffs. I could pick up solos pretty handy, as I had a bit of an ear for it. I could pick up a song in a couple of minutes and have the solo down in five minutes.

The singing didn't come until later and it didn't come as easy because I was a bit shy. It wasn't until I was around seventeen that I sang in front of anybody and that was at the Yoplait Song

Contest organised by 2FM. The contest gave me great confidence, but it was very tough on me, having to get up there and sing live in the studio and then with the contest going out live on national radio. But it was worth it, because I came second and won a ghetto blaster! The song I sang was called 'Cardboard City'. It was one of the first songs I ever wrote. I thought I should have won, but some country song won it. But when I saw this huge ghetto blaster I said to myself, "I think I'll stick at this". It was great!

I've quite a few influences, including Luke Kelly. Christy Moore gave me great encouragement too and I'm a huge fan of his. Sinead O'Connor, Shane McGowan, I have a good few heroes like that. There are moments too that stick out in my memory and that inspired me along the way. When I heard Luke Kelly sing 'Raglan Road' it moved me to tears. Bob Marley had an album called *Talkin' Blues* and Peter Tosh was on it and I had a few smokes listening to it and I thought, "Jesus, that's out of this world!" Hearing Christy Moore singing a song about Francis Hughes was also very moving, and then The Pogues' 'Fairytale of New York' made me feel very warm inside. So there are lots of songs and records and performances that have stirred me.

I'm very happy doing what I love doing, but it can be a struggle financially and it can be hard to survive. But the main thing is that I'm happy now."

FAVOURITE SINGER: Sinead O'Connor

FAVOURITE ALBUM: *Talkin' Blues* by Bob Marley

FAVOURITE SONG: 'Rainy Night in Soho' by The Pogues

15

DAMIEN RICE

Singer-songwriter Damien Rice is 29 and was born and raised in Celbridge, Co Kildare. 2002 was a truly amazing year for this platinum-selling artist, with appearances at some of the year's biggest music festivals at home and abroad, alongside numerous TV appearances, all serving to excite his ever-growing fan base. Damien's debut album, *O*, crashed into the top 10 the first week of release and provided him with three top-thirty singles. Immediately greeted with widespread public and critical acclaim, the album was hailed as one of the foremost albums of the year. According to Irish rock bible *Hot Press*, "*O* ebbs and flows gracefully through some of the most heart-wrenching, uplifting, sweepingly romantic and darkly contemplative tracks in his repertoire. It throbs with sheer humanity and bloody-minded honesty in the face of emotional debris . . . absolutely stunning!" Damien also garnered top-drawer reviews from some of Britain's most respected music critics. The *Daily Telegraph* described him as 'a young singer-song-writer capable of touching the parts most of his contemporaries will never reach'.

"This is really sad! The first song I learned to play was 'Living Next Door To Alice' by Smokie. My dad used to play in a pub band. He was mad into Smokie, so he taught me the chords for it, A, D and E, on the guitar. Then I got a book and I learned G, E minor, C and E and I learned to play 'Stand By Me', the Ben E King hit. From then on I just picked up things myself.

I wrote my first song when I was about thirteen or fourteen, and I continued through a couple of years of writing influenced by this song or that song. Things changed though when I was living in a house in Ardclough with a band I used to play with called Juniper. It was a big old barracks with big fat brick walls. I had been asked by our management to write some up-tempo singles for the record company. I was naive enough to say, "OK, sure, no problem." As I saw it, this was our job, to provide the right product for the record company to sell. I spent three days trying to write some fast songs that I thought would make good upbeat singles. On the third day I was sitting on my bed when I realised I'd written a load of rubbish just for the sake of it. It all sounded forced. I was so frustrated with what I'd written that I threw my guitar angrily off the bed and it bounced off the floor and hit off a radiator. Assuming I had damaged the guitar I just knelt on the floor in frustration. And then I looked at the window and saw that it had started raining. To make matters worse the house was fairly isolated so I couldn't go anywhere. The rain just got heavier and heavier and I became even more depressed. I felt a failure, not being able to write to order. Without thinking I reached out for the guitar. I just strummed it in open tuning and my hand just fell on to this chord and within about eight minutes the words and music of my song, 'Eskimo', seemed to fall out of nowhere - just fell out, right there and then! It was there so suddenly and so easily after three days of worrying and feeling under pressure, without me even thinking about writing a song.

From then on I've never tried to write, I just let it come. In fact, the best songs I've written came really quickly. Those that turned out mediocre were the ones that were a struggle and those that are crap are ones I just spent ages at. That just seems to be the way it works with me. Worrying about it never comes to anything of any consequence.

When I was in primary school I wanted to be a scientist. My best friend wanted to be a rock star and I slagged him off. We both sang in the choir. I've always sung. I'd had a drum kit when I was younger but I was crap at the drums. I never really got to practise them in the house because they were too loud. But the minute I picked up a guitar I went, "Whoa! This works." I could do two things at the same time, sing and play, two things that come natural to me.

My first ever gig on stage was in secondary school with the first band I was in called Wanted Not Needed. I think we did a gig for Spanish students who'd come over to Celbridge for the summer. We just stood there doing U2 covers.

Prince has definitely been a major influence on me. He was one of my teenage favourites, especially the Purple Rain album. I thought he was really cool, very talented and with songs that were sexy and honest. Now I'm into people like Nina Simone, Leonard Cohen, Tom Waits, but that could change again. The Frames are without doubt my favourite Irish band. They definitely inspired me. During an emotional time in my life I was recording the *O* album and spending some time around them, going to their gigs, doing support for them and getting a great reaction from their audience. It was a magical time and when I hear their albums, *Dance the Devil* and *For The Birds*, I get emotional.

I used to be quite ambitious about success, and still am to an extent, but my understanding of success has totally changed.

My main goal now is to continue as I've done without letting success change my 'I don't give a damn' attitude, because the more successful you get the more responsibility you get. When I wrote *O* I had no responsibilities. It was that freedom and that wildness and that chaos that allowed me to record the way I did. Although I would like to take the music wherever it wants to go, I would like to remain wild and free and stupid and chaotic. Success is being happy with yourself, with what you've done, with your life, with your friends and how you treat people."

16

DANIEL O'DONNELL

Daniel O'Donnell is one of the most internationally popular solo singers to have emerged from Ireland in recent years, a star instantly recognised by the mere mention of his first name. Born in Donegal, Daniel is renowned as one of the hardest working singers in show business. From sell-out tours to chart-topping albums, he has a remarkable track record stretching back over nearly three decades. His fund-raising efforts have generated substantial amounts of money for his favourite charity, the Romanian Challenge Appeal. In 2002 he was awarded an Honorary MBE for his 'services to the music industry', while his own television show on the BBC has drawn record audiences. Nor is his fan base confined to these shores - it extends across the Atlantic to America and beyond to New Zealand and Australia where his albums sell in massive quantities.

" When I was young I remember being at home listening to the many informal singsongs that used to take place there. As I was growing up I can vaguely remember different individuals singing, including many people we knew who would have lived away from Ireland for a time. So when they came home, either for holidays or for good, there would be lots of singsongs and parties. We would also go to hear music in the Marquee in Dungloe.

I think my first serious introduction to music would have been through my sister Margo. She was herself starting to record as an artist and I can remember about 1968 when her first record was released. I was becoming aware of that aspect of music and the business side of it too. Dana winning the Eurovision Song Contest in 1970 with 'All Kinds Of Everything' was a very big thing for the young people of that era. Eurovision was a really big annual event for pop music fans back then, and the fact that Dana was the first artist to win it for Ireland caused enormous excitement. I remember it all very, very clearly. I was born in 1961 so when Dana won the competition I was only about nine, but I was old enough to be impressed by her and her achievement. Her victory got great coverage and it was all over the television and radio for weeks.

I never really thought much of becoming a singer when I was growing up. In fact, from a fairly early age I thought I would like to become a schoolteacher. I started in the regional college to do business studies in 1980, but I began to think seriously about music from around my mid-teens, just quietly thinking about what I might do with it, but not speaking to anybody about it. I was singing a lot back then, because everywhere I went people would ask me to sing, like at weddings and in the church, all that sort of thing.

I never really thought I would ever do it full-time, nor even part-time at the weekend like a lot of musicians did at that time. But when I hit my late teens I decided to give it a go. I felt that I really wanted to try it and I'd rather try and fail than spend the rest of my life wondering about what might have been.

While I was in college in Galway, my sister had a band on the road. So I spoke to her about it. I had a good talk with her and she eventually took me on and I travelled with her for a couple of years. There were no demands on me at all, I just sang a few songs every night, but that period gave me the opportunity to observe the music business at first-hand and I realised how much I enjoyed being part of it. Before long, I realised that I really wanted to try to make some sort of go of it on my own. So in 1983 I left her band and made my first record, which was 'My Donegal Shore' and 'Stand Beside Me'. I started my own band that same year.

I remember the first gig with my own band. It took place in Dungloe. Sure, we had our whole set sung by 1 o'clock and we had to sing till 2 o'clock, so we sang the whole set a second time! It was nerve-wracking in a way, because I was starting out on my own, but I believe the only way to start is to go and do it, to get on with it. Instead of waiting for something to come to you, you have to go to it. I think a lot of people sit and wait for their break to come to them but it doesn't happen that way. It may come to you if you're out there looking for it, but it certainly won't come looking to find you. Even now with television programmes like *Pop Idol* and all that sort of thing, you still have to go and do the work. But you must believe in what you do too. I've always believed in myself, even when I know that not many believed in what I was doing, mainly because I was singing songs that a lot of people had discarded. But I loved those songs and I loved singing and I believed very strongly and that's the secret.

But it was very difficult for me probably up until 1986. In fact I seriously thought of giving it all up at the end of 1985 because it just wasn't working out. We were getting no crowds. But then it suddenly happened, almost like switching on a light. I started with my present band in March of 1986. Sean Reilly, who still manages me, became my manager at the same time and I signed up to Ritz Records and we found instant success!

One recent memory sticks out. I don't know whether it's just because it was recent, but I did an inspirational show in the Helix in Dublin. I had a full orchestra, an 80-piece choir and a gospel group who travel with us as well as my own band. That concert was just amazing. It was so uplifting to have all those musicians and singers on the same stage. It was an incredible night and it made me realise how lucky I am to have had these opportunities and to have all of this around me. I had started out so humbly. I couldn't believe I was the centre of it all. It was a truly wonderful experience. I don't know if I could ever repeat that, it was so exceptional.

I love singing the inspirational material as well as the other stuff. I sing a lot of different types of music, but there was something very special about that night."

FAVOURITE ALBUM:
It would have to be something from Abba, perhaps their *Greatest Hits*, because that was my era.

FAVOURITE SINGER:
The country singer, Loretta Lynn.

17

DAVID AGNEW

Born in Dublin, David Agnew first studied the piano, recorder and guitar before taking up the oboe at the age of seventeen. Now a world-renowned oboist, Agnew is best known for his work on the film *The Mission*, with its theme 'Gabriel's Oboe' enjoying the kind of chart success rare for an instrumental work. Agnew has also recorded with several revered Irish artists, including The Chieftains.

" My most vivid and earliest musical memory was in 1963, when I was six. My father, the tenor Arthur Agnew, was singing the Mario Lanza part in an RTE production of *The Student Prince*. The glamorous costumes, the fabulous music and the excitement of live performance have stayed with me to this day. Watching the footage, which I've since transferred to video, brings back magic memories.

He used to sing every Sunday on a live Old Time Music Hall radio show, *Town Hall Tonight*. I listened to it through a tiny earpiece under the bedcovers on a crystal radio I'd assembled myself. It seemed so exciting, like spying, and I kept quiet in case anyone heard me. Even when I was older I listened to radio under the bedclothes to great shows like *Get an Earful of This* on RTE, and Kid Jensen on Radio Luxembourg. I often woke with a sore ear from the earpiece!

My father was a world-class tenor who should have been a contender, but being the eldest of eight from a relatively poor background he joined the Civil Service at eighteen and stayed there for 43 years. Music for him was always a joy, an escape from the humdrum daily pen-pushing. He had great musical friends, and most of his social life revolved around musical evenings in different houses.

My mother sang too, and loved making food for parties. I loved the camaraderie, the fun, the music and the reassurance that "there was always food on the table" when music was played. We had many such nights in our house, with well-known and brilliant musicians doing their party-pieces. There always seemed to be joy in the music-making.

I remember three gigs specifically because of the impression they made on me. The first was a Schools Concert by the RTE Symphony Orchestra in the St Francis Xavier Hall in Sherrard Street, coincidentally the same venue used for *Town Hall Tonight*. I was twelve and wrote an appreciation of the concert, which was read out, to the orchestra at a subsequent rehearsal where I shook hands with the Conductor, Leader and Manager. I was made to feel very welcome.

The second gig was a small amateur performance of *Messiah* by the Dublin Baroque Players, still an exceptionally talented bunch of musicians. My father sang the solo tenor part and I remember thinking that that was what I really wanted to do, to play in front of an orchestra. But I was only thirteen and didn't know what I was going to play. I played piano but hated it. I had just discovered the guitar and wanted to be Jimi Hendrix, Eric Clapton or Rory Gallagher. I was quite a good recorder player too, but didn't see a big future in it, and I didn't discover the oboe until I was seventeen.

The third gig I remember vividly was my first playing-paying gig. I was sixteen and played electric guitar in *Viva Mexico* with the Whitehall Amateur Musical Society. I was paid £4 each night for four nights. I thought I was rich and really in the music business.

When I left Coláiste Mhuire in Parnell Square at eighteen I had been playing oboe for only a year and wasn't very good. I wanted to be an artist and got an A in my Leaving exam, but I reasoned that artists only depicted the way they saw things, whereas a scientist asked why things were the way they were. So I did a B Sc (Hons) in botany. I played oboe at night and the professional work paid my fees and social expenses. I also got Arts Council scholarships for three years, which gave me a chance to study at international master-classes overseas. But when I finished my primary degree I still didn't think I was good enough on oboe to be a full-time professional, so I did a M Sc in tree biology. I loved the fieldwork.

It was during this time I got a French Government scholar-ship to study in Indonesia, the South of France, Florida and Harvard University for a Ph D. But a half-hour before I was to board the plane I decided I was in love and wanted to be a musician. And it's been downhill ever since!

My future wife was playing Nancy in *Oliver* and I was in the orchestra. I knew then that I didn't want to be anywhere but with her. To be a musician was an easy decision to make, as I was tired spending so much time researching, always on my own. I longed for the whole live concert experience, and I don't regret a day of my career decision.

I have had thousands of wonderful moments in music. There are times when the moment is absolutely perfect and you want it to last forever. The experience of that moment brings you closer to something you can't explain. It may be God for some, or just a glimpse of what we hope Paradise to be, but it's a gift to have in your heart and to help others to understand.

My most precious moments include playing for Celine Dion when she won Eurovision in Dublin in 1988. It was a beautiful experience; playing for the great actor Ray McAnally's funeral in the Pro-Cathedral, Dublin, in 1989. 'Gabriel's Oboe', the theme from *The Mission* in which he starred, was his favourite piece of music and I had just recorded it with Frank McNamara. It was an honour to play it for him. That piece changed my life. It has given me a reason to play the oboe all over the world.

Playing for the first performance of *Riverdance* at Eurovision in 1994 was an extraordinary moment in music. Those seven minutes helped Ireland spread its culture far and wide, and I've been carried on the crest of that wave to America, Japan, Korea, Israel, Egypt and many other places;

There have been many precious and unforgettable times on-stage with artists such as Perry Como, Rod Stewart, REM, Van Morrison, Sinead O'Connor, Ronnie Drew, Finbar Furey, Jimmy Galway, Phil Coulter, Mary Black, Jimmy MacCarthy, Sir George Martin, The Chieftains, Brian Kennedy, my Dad, my wife Adele King (Twink) and, probably my most favourite voice of all, Tommy Fleming.

When you have a lot of work you feel on top of the world, invincible and rich, all totally untrue, but you convince yourself. When there is no work, or you are ill but have to work, you can feel frustrated with the music business and look at other possibilities. Usually this passes as soon as the phone rings with the next engagement!

I've sometimes felt frustrated at my lack of progress in international territories, despite so many phone-calls, meetings, CDs sent, CVs posted, all often for nothing. But you have to remind yourself you're there for the long haul. It's a rollercoaster of emotions for me, but it adds to the quality of the emotion in my playing and I try to use it in a positive way."

18

DAVID HOLMES

David Holmes was born in Belfast in 1969. A hugely successful DJ and music producer, he has four critically acclaimed albums to his name, *This Film's Crap Let's Slash The Seats* (1995), *Let's Get Killed* (1997), *Bow Down to the Exit Sign* (2000) and *Come Get It, I Got It* (2002). Elsewhere his innovative work on various movie soundtracks includes *Oceans 11*, *Out of Sight* and *Analyze That*. More recently Holmes formed a band called The Free Association. Their debut album was released in 2002. An enormous music lover, his personal record collection provides many inspirations for the various projects he simultaneously works on.

"My first experience of music can be described in two words, 'Punk Rock'. Like the Sex Pistols, the Clash and the Damned, X-Ray Specs. That was the first thing to shoot me; the first thing I really got excited about. I hadn't a clue and didn't know why because I didn't understand a word of what they were saying or what they were singing about. I just loved the energy, the noise and the racket that was being made. You can't really analyze that when you're really young, but I just liked it.

Back then in Belfast there weren't many opportunities. I was always involved in music for music's sake. I used to go to different clubs and in my teens I really got into the Mod movement, rhythm-and-blues and really obscure jazz records. I followed bands like the Small Faces, The Creation. That got me into DJing.

So I started DJing and the whole thing just developed from there really and I never looked back. I was getting paid for something that I really loved doing. That led through the late 80's where there was so much music around: soul, punk, reggae, hip hop. It was all there on one dance floor. So it was a real education, I was having my education and I didn't even know it.

Music never even seemed like I was working. I never turned around and said I want to be a producer or I want to be a musician. All these things just happened because I never really thought it was possible. It seemed like a far-off land. Things like that couldn't really be possible. The whole acid house movement gave me the platform to go into a recording studio, with an idea and an engineer and turn it into a reality. The whole thing was really non-musical. It was really rhythmical and had a real synther-pulse to the whole thing. It was very much about the energy and when I started introducing samples to my work that's what gave it its emotion.

I followed my heart and followed my gut instinct and always tried to make music that was true to me. That's how I fell into the whole soundtrack thing because when I was making music, the press would say how cinematic they thought it was and that's something that never struck me. It was just something that was very natural. So I started looking into film sound-tracks as a form of inspiration, watching loads of old films and taking my inspiration from that. I was fusing that with drum machines and analogue synthesisers and coming up with something that was identifiably mine rather then making music that sounded like someone else's.

There's several people that have been a huge influence on my life musically. From Andrew Weatherall to Brian Eno to Pete Meadon. Pete Meadon managed the High Numbers that went on to be The Who. He was a completely obsessed fan of music, clothes and the whole lifestyle that was modism. Different people for different reasons inspire me. Weatherall was an anti-musician. He would kick a door to get a kick drum sound. He was very unconventional in the way he made music. I'm much more interested in unconventional producers rather than people who know every single trick in the book. Brian Eno once said that a lot of the best music he had heard in guitar-based music and in avant garde music was made by dabblers and amateurs because they didn't have any pre-conceived notion of how the song was going to finish up. It was a matter of getting in among it all and feeling the whole thing and just throwing ideas into the pot. It's great for people who don't play musical instruments.

I remember playing at my first-ever gig, I can remember it clearly. The DJ didn't turn up and I had a good record collection so they asked me would I do it. So, I went home and got my records. I had a dud bus ticket and a pound for a pint and I left that night with 15 pounds in my pocket. I went down the next day to Caroline Music in Belfast and bought three albums at 3.99 each.

I have had so many moments where I've realised I love what I do. The main reason why is that music isn't a job. It should never be treated as a job; sometimes you can't escape the fact that you have to deal with certain aspects of it like the accounting side of it, for instance. But sometimes you have to do it. Music as an art form, it's not work. Sitting in a recording studio making music to me is the best thing in the world."

19

DAVID KITT

In 2001 David Kitt's smoothly cool album, *The Big Romance*, was received warmly and excitedly by audiences and critics alike. 'Song From Hope St. (Brooklyn, NY)', with its wonderfully tongue-in-cheek animated video, and 'You Know What I Want To Know' graduated from being live favourites to singles acclaimed by the growing army of fans who follow this talented singer from Dublin. David's debut *Small Moments* had been recorded in his bedroom, but *The Big Romance* benefits from being recorded in a 'proper' studio, thereby allowing David to better illustrate the electronic side of his music. Either way, Kitt's recordings have all been applauded for their technical accomplishments while still retaining the intimate feeling of his music. He has also grown in stature on the 'gigging' front, having toured extensively with the likes of Arab Strap, Tindersticks, Kathryn Williams, Beth Orton and Television.

" The sound of the guitar is something I have always associated with great comfort. My dad started teaching me when I was about seven or eight. Initially I didn't take to it. I was a bit lazy, because the lessons would be at half-past nine on a Saturday morning and it meant missing *Football Focus* and a lot of other good Saturday morning TV programmes. So I wasn't overly enthusiastic at first. But later on, maybe when I was ten, I just started playing it and making up my own songs, writing bits and pieces, and that's when I really started getting into it.

The first gig I ever went to was Spandau Ballet in the RDS in Dublin. But my first special memory of an amazing gig was Lou Reed opening for U2 in Croke Park in 1987. I was just getting into Lou at the time and I had his greatest hits album and I was just getting into the Velvet Underground.

Music was always something that I did, but it wasn't until I recorded my first EP Small Moments (I had recorded about seven before I actually released one!), that I began to think that this is really good stuff and that maybe I could do it full time.

Up until that point it was just something that I did all the time. It was just a habit, like an addiction, something that you just have to do to survive. It wasn't until quite late in life that I thought that I could make a career out of it. It's a great comfort to be able to make music and to be able to work on four tracks and eight tracks and hear different tracks together and see all the possibilities of the writing and recording process. I guess early on I started getting into Indie music through bands like REM. Then I got into stuff like Dinosaur Junior, Sonic Youth and My Bloody Valentine. That was all very exciting to me. For the first time I was finding my own tastes in music, and this was stuff that nobody else seemed to have. I felt as if I was just discovering this music myself. That all played a part, but I reckon the biggest influence in terms of what I do now came in the late nineties with the release of De La Soul's *Three Feet High And Rising* album and A Tribe Called Quest's first album. Those two records had a big influence on me because they were really melodic hip-hop and kind of tonal. There was less of a cultural barrier than I would have felt with a lot of stuff like NWA and Public Enemy. I found the others a lot more accessible. Then I got more and more into soul, reggae, ska and black music in general. That's when I started exploring further into different genres of music. I started with Bob Marley and Otis Redding and then started to find more obscure stuff.

When I was younger, for years I wanted to be a lawyer. I studied economics for four years, but I had no real intention of becoming an economist. But I thought that a knowledge of it would be helpful in relation to certain things that I was interested in, like the economies of less developed countries, income inequality and so on. But I never really saw myself getting into any of it in any big way. Then I studied music technology and that helped me to get into what I'm doing now.

One of the best gigs I ever did was at the Witnness Festival at Fairyhouse racecourse. That was definitely in my top five gigs of all time. It was just amazing to hear so many people singing back to me songs that I had written. It's like you take something you wrote in your bedroom before you had a record deal and all of a sudden there's ten thousand people singing it. That's obviously an incredible feeling, and the warmth from the audience and the fact that it was a celebration for everyone made it really memorable. Everyone was kind of going "Wow, this is an Irish act and he's done really well". Everybody was quite proud and I certainly felt very proud after what was a great day.

I'm privileged to get the chance to do this full time. I'd like to be able to make a few quid from what I'm doing and try to have a bit of financial independence which will allow me to build my own studio. That's one of my main goals. I'd like to do less touring and do more producing of records and more recording. I'd like to focus more on that side of it. That would be my dream, but my main goal at the moment is to make a record that I feel would sit comfortably in my top ten records of all time."

FAVOURITE ARTIST: There's just too many. It's too hard to pick one.

FAVOURITE ALBUM: The debut album by the Velvet Underground and Nico.

FAVOURITE MOMENT: Playing at Witnness 2001 to a crowd of ten thousand.

20

DERVISH
Cathy Jordan, lead singer

Roscommon-born Cathy Jordan is the lead singer with Irish traditional band Dervish. After joining the band in 1991, she sang lead vocals on their first album, *Harmony Hill*, which was released in 1992. The album won widespread critical acclaim and was described by many as "a landmark Irish traditional album". Many albums, tours and gigs later, Dervish are now regarded as one of Ireland's premier traditional Irish groups, having performed world-wide to ecstatic audiences.

" Thinking back to it now, my father singing was my first memory of music. He was regarded around my home parish as a great singer of ballads and traditional songs. I remember we got a gramophone sent over from the United States in a parcel when I was only about seven. It was a wind-up one, a huge thing, and it was put in the backroom of the house. I hadn't thought it was possible to be able to hear music from a little round disc, to stick it on, put a needle on it and out would come such wonderful sounds. To my ears and eyes it was amazing. We used to beg for more records to be bought, and we had loads of old 78s. We had the McPeake family, the Flanagan Brothers and Michael Coleman. But for as much Irish music as we listened to, there was an equal amount of American country music as well, including the legendary Hank Williams. It's funny that all the way through my childhood the two went hand-in-hand. You will find that a lot of Irish families would have had the same mix, and American country music is very popular in Ireland even today, more popular than some people would give it credit for. There are a lot of closet country music and bluegrass music fans out there. But then bluegrass and traditional music are linked and there's a funny marriage between the two for a lot of people. So our house was no different in its musical experiences from many other Irish houses.

It wasn't until later that I thought of taking on music as a career. When I was nine I wanted to be a nun, but that soon wore off me! I think that it was because this cousin of my father was a nun in Australia and worked out in the Philippines for a while. She used to come and visit us every year. I was very devout at the time. I was just so in awe of the fact that she travelled and that she wore lovely medals and that she was holy. Thankfully the phase only lasted a year or so before I got sense. But from a singing point of view, the rest of the family and all my friends noticed my serious fascination with performing before I did. They were convinced that I had a career ahead of me because I always wanted to be heard above everybody else and always wanted to perform. I just had that drive in me for it. I absolutely loved it and had very little interest in anything else except learning songs and singing them. When I asked my mother, God rest her, before she died, about when I started singing, she said that I would make up my own songs in the cot before I could talk. She knew it even then and it's funny now hearing stories like that. When you are living through it, you don't see it as clearly as others who are looking on and taking it all in.

I found out from a very early stage that this business is a bit like a rollercoaster. You might be on the down a while and feel like nothing is going right. It might last a day or two because you didn't like the last gig or your head wasn't in gear for it. But I always know that it will get better. But sometimes you can be as low as it's possible to be, and at other times as high as you can be. I love not knowing what the day is going to bring or what the week ahead will be like. Sometimes music makes me as happy as I could ever wish to be. It can make me frustrated one day, and the next day I can feel the exact opposite. But I've never wanted to give it up.

When I think of influences, my neighbour, who was much older then me by a good ten or fifteen years, was the first person I ever saw playing a guitar live right in front of me. He was a big fan of people like Bob Dylan, Tom Waits, Leonard Cohen, Guy Clarke and Rodney Crowell, and he introduced me to all these artists at a very young age. He was the one with all the records by Luke Kelly and *sean-nós* singers like Nicholas Tobín. In fact the first Nicholas Tobín record I heard had a major impact on me. When you have a record and you talk about it to other people, they will tell you about another one and your knowledge of music snowballs.

There are several musical areas in which I would now have to admit that that neighbour was responsible for encouraging my interest. He also taught me how to play the guitar and I sang a lot of sessions with him. All those people he introduced me to became influences on me subsequently.

I rarely went to a gig until I was about seventeen. I came from a very rural part of the world where extra-curricular activity meant working on the bog and the meadow. We didn't really have much opportunity for luxuries like going to concerts. But my sister brought me to a festival where Dé Danann were playing and I just thought it was the best thing I had ever seen. Dolores Keane was singing with them, and Frankie Gavin and the boys were playing away and I just thought it was fantastic, which it was. Looking back now, with all my years of experience since then, it still seems as brilliant to me now as it was then."

21

THE DIVINE COMEDY

Neil Hannon, songwriter

As a songwriter and the driving force behind The Divine Comedy, Neil Hannon has become one of Ireland's most respected singer-songwriters. Born in Derry in 1970, Neil's main influences include Jacques Brel, Scott Walker and Michael Nyman. Since forming The Divine Comedy in Enniskillen at the age of eighteen, he has released eight albums and scored numerous international hit singles with songs like 'National Express'. He also wrote the signature tune for the acclaimed television series, *Father Ted*.

" *Jungle Book* is my most distinctive memory of music from back around 1972-1973. That was the only record we were allowed to play in our house on our very old-fashioned record player. I'm sure you can see its influence in the music that I've written (ha-ha!). There haven't been many sound-tracks as good as it. There's pure quality and inventiveness running all the way through it. I don't even know who brought the record into the house. It was just there, like part of the furniture.

Apart from that, in the early days it was our Bechstein grand piano in the drawing room which had a huge effect on me. I was so fascinated by it that I apparently once took a hammer to the keys. I don't remember doing this, but I've been often told with great gusto by my father that the chips in the ivories were created by me with that hammer. Maybe it was the only way I could reach the keys!

I started showing a serious interest in the piano when my dad, who was a clergyman, sent me to piano lessons. He was a big influence in getting me into music; he was the only person in the family who could actually play anything. He was a pianist, and a very good one too. My grandmother always loved to tell me that he could have been a concert pianist had he not gone into the clergy. I'm not sure whether she would have preferred it if he had, but I doubt it! He would play the piano at home regularly, but especially before the services on a Sunday when he was trying to clear his head, and we would hear the music of classical composers like Bach and Debussy emanating from the front room.

Apart from my dad, there was the enormous influence of my elder brothers who had discovered all this 'crazy pop music' before I had. They were always very keen to impress upon me that they knew much more than I did. Through them I was weaned on *Top of the Pops* and BBC Radio One from a very young age. I think that encouraged a love of ridiculous seventies pop. It was a great education for me, because I think that the late seventies in a way was a golden era for pop music in Britain. I vividly remember acts like The Pretenders, Elvis Costello, The Jam, Gary Numan, right up to the Human League and all the synthesiser pop bands that I really adored. It was a fantastic mix and, apart from the style of it all, there was some amazing songwriting going on which diminished somewhat in the years afterwards.

But the first thing I ever wanted to be was a car designer. I think that was partly because of the whole De Lorean thing going on in Derry at the time. They made these incredible-looking cars there, just like the one featured in the Michael J Fox movie, *Back to the Future*. I was very much taken by the sky wing doors, and all the cars that I designed had gold wing doors. But my love of cars gradually gave way to music. I could have been as young as eleven when I thought, "Hmmmm, that music looks like fun". I gradually persuaded myself through my teenage years that music was such an unavoidable attraction that in time I wondered how anybody could think I could have done anything else. I knew I couldn't have done anything else.

There are so many great moments, but every time you come off stage you say to yourself, "That's why I do it". Searching through the murky depths of my memory, I can remember the moment when I realised that I was happy and content with what I was doing. It was back in 1996 when I was travelling in a taxi in Paris and the record company phoned me to tell me that 'Something For The Weekend', the first single we released from our third album, had gone into the charts at number 14 or 15. I thought, "Oh my lord I've actually achieved my only real goal, to be invited on *Top of the Pops*." Anything after that was going to be a bonus. Since then I've been kind of drifting and on a high. But I've been amazingly lucky to have been able to make a career out of writing and playing the music I love."

FAVOURITE SONG: 'Ev'ry Time We Say Goodbye' by Cole Porter (My favourite song today, but it changes daily). My favourite used to be 'Moon River', but I've said it so often that I've become sick of it by now!

BIGGEST INFLUENCE: My single biggest influence is Scott

Walker. He had lots of hits in the sixties with the Walker Brothers and then afterwards as a solo singer. Maybe he's been too much of an influence on me, but once he got in there he basically changed the way I sang.

22

DOMINIC KIRWAN

Born in Omagh, Co Tyrone in 1960, Dominic Kirwan has been cited as one of Ireland's most dynamic and successful Country music artists. Since forming his first band over twenty years ago, he has released over five albums and several live videos. He has toured extensively across the world, and such is his live reputation that he has been invited on various tours to share stages with renowned Country music artists of the calibre of Charley Pride, Kenny Rogers and the late Tammy Wynette.

" My initial introduction to music would have come through my background in Irish dancing. There was always folk and traditional music in and around the home when I was growing up. I have a strong memory of my mother who was a pianist who played in local pantomimes and variety shows. She would have been into the classical side of music, so that was another musical influence around the home. Looking back now, all this was probably something that

I really didn't much notice at the time but just took for granted.

There's a story that my mother told me about a Christian Brother who stopped her on the street when I was about six years of age. He mentioned to her that he and others thought that I had a really good singing voice. So, after that conversation, anything that came to our attention, be it the school choir, a music competition or local *feis* competitions, I would seem to pop up in them.

My development as a performer was gradual, making slow but steady progress along the way. To me it seems that a path had been set out for me almost before I started. I never really planned it out or even thought much about it when I was a kid, but now that I look back at it seems there was some kind of destiny working for me. I can't actually sit down and say that at some early age I had decided that I was going to be a singer when I grew up and that this was what my life was going to be about. It was always this gradual thing of one thing leading to another.

When I was about fourteen or fifteen I thought that I wanted to be an engineer, and so I started to head in that direction as far as my schooling went. I enrolled in the local technical college and started an engineering course, but at the same time I had become involved with a local band, a group of lads that I knew around Omagh. No matter what career options I might have looked at, music was never far away from me and I even had a go at talent competitions that took place around the area. It was as if I was still being attracted back along that particular path and some powerful force was pulling me away from every other consideration about what I might do for the rest of my life.

Musically, the biggest influence on me would probably have been my mother's support. She was fantastic. In her own time as a public performer she told me that, although she played piano regularly at local productions, she would always insist that she would not be seen sitting out front. She would play the piano from the side of the stage instead. She later insisted that if any of her kids were ever going to go down that road of playing music in public she would insist that they would be seen and get the recognition they deserved for their achievements. So I enjoyed her backing from an early age.

I was like any other kid born in the sixties, growing up in the seventies and really, really listening to what was happening in music through that time. I was big into the really good voices of the day. I was a big fan of Tom Jones, for example. Although I was very young at that time I was very much into his type of music.

When I was in my teens, I used to work as a waiter in the GAA club in the town. Wednesday nights were very big nights for folk music and a lot of top bands would come and play, with many of the local, and less well-known, bands to be heard at the weekend. This brought me into closer contact with that kind of music, and I saw many of the folksy type of acts of that time, performers like Danny Doyle and Johnny McEvoy. They were still in the early days of their careers and I was always amazed by the impression they made on me from up there on the stage.

From my later years I have a vivid memory of the singer Rita MacNeil who had enjoyed a very big hit with 'The Working Man'. I was on my way to do a gig somewhere in the North of Ireland at the time. She was playing in the Rialto Theatre in Derry and I was asked to come along, but I knew I couldn't stay too long at her show. But I stayed long enough to see that she had an amazing light show. That's one of the strongest memories I have with me to this day. That show made me realise that you have to look at all aspects of your stage show. Singing well isn't enough; you have to look at the visual aspect, the whole showbiz and presentation side of things.

Another great memory is of going to see the Simon and Garfunkel reunion tour, which came to the RDS in Dublin. What a great show that was, one I'll never forget!

I don't have any one big defining moment that would or could sum up my career. There have been so many different occasions, like when I got my first recording contract with Ritz Records back in 1989. That was a big moment for me, especially realising that not many acts would get a contract like that. Other special memories include my 1990 meeting with Charley Pride and touring with him for five weeks. Touring with Tammy Wynette and Kenny Rogers were also special times, as was recording in Nashville, Tennessee."

23

DON BAKER

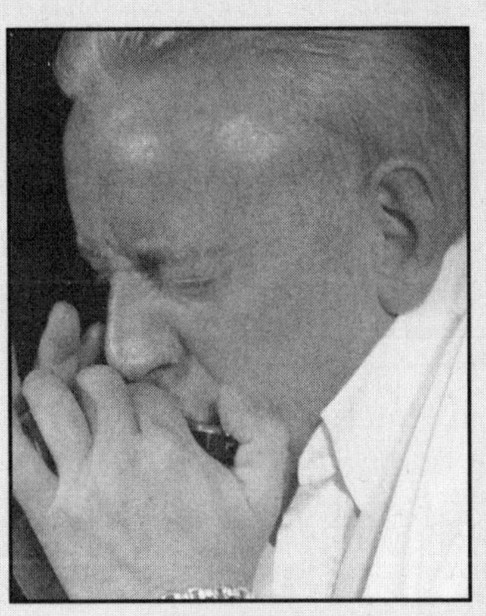

Don Baker was born in the Dublin suburb of Whitehall in 1950. A renowned blues guitarist, harmonica player and a singer with a rare emotional depth, Don has been on the road entertaining audiences all over the world for more than thirty years. Once described by Bono as "the greatest harmonica player in the world", Don has played alongside legends of the calibre of international rock star Joe Cocker and the late Irish blues legend, Rory Gallagher. He is also the author of several instruction books on playing the harmonica which have been translated into several languages and proven to be hugely popular all over the world. Don is held in such esteem by the world's leading harmonica connoisseurs that he is regularly invited to adjudicate at the bi-annual World Harmonica Championships. His musical adventures and his fight against alcoholism and other demons are graphically described in the book, *The Winner In Me,* by Jackie Hayden.

"One of my first introductions to music was listening to a guy playing the harmonica when I was a child in hospital. He had tuberculosis of the spine, so he couldn't do very much except read and play the instrument because he had to lie on his back all of the time. It was the first time I had ever heard the instrument, and my ears pricked up as if it was some kind of awakening. I believe that something in the sound of it touched my soul when I heard it that first time. The size of the instrument or the shape of it didn't bother me at all. I wasn't the sort of kid who was into big drums or shiny red guitars, it was the sound of the harmonica that won me over. In fact I find it extraordinary that such a small instrument can be used to evoke such a range of real human emotions.

After my mother agreed to bring one into the hospital for me I started to play it as often as I could. I'm sure I drove some of the other patients crazy! I took to it straight away and I thought it was great fun altogether being able to pick out tunes on it that I heard on the radio. What appealed to me most was that there was nobody standing over me telling me to learn this or learn that. I also found that I liked performing in front of an audience, no matter if it was only one or two kids. When I was in a rehabilitation centre in Bray in County Wicklow I decided to take it more seriously and turn it into a profession. I was about nineteen and I'd had my first introduction to playing guitar too. I decided that this was what I wanted to dedicate my life to.

Another event that made it a whole new world for me was the first gig I ever went to in Mahers of Moore Street in Dublin to see a band called Blues House. It was there I met a great harmonica player called Eamon Murray. It was around that time that I'd been introduced to blues music and it had really clicked with me.

Another guy who really influenced me was Richard Euzell

who lived near me in the inner city of Dublin. He was a huge influence and he really changed my life simply by introducing me to this magnificent world of blues music. He also encouraged me to read Woody Guthrie's book, *Bound For Glory*, in which the folk-singer wrote of his adventures travelling all over America. I think I may have stolen some of Richie's dreams in a way, because after reading the Guthrie book I busked here, there and anywhere, just like Woody had done.

Richie went to work for CIE because he wanted the security of a full-time job, whereas I wasn't too pushed about things like that. I started travelling around Europe and soon became convinced that travel is very good for you. It's very educational to see how other people live, to learn at first-hand how traditions, languages, religions and beliefs come about. Those experiences sealed performing for me as a career.

But, although playing music was everything to me, there were times when I wouldn't have any money to buy presents and stuff at Christmas. When you're a struggling musician you don't earn much money. I didn't earn much for about fifteen years, maybe more. I earned enough for food and travel, but I certainly wouldn't have needed a team of accountants!

I see playing the music, writing my books and my videos as like doing a dance, doing your own thing. I'm very lucky to be able to earn my living from something that I love. That's what success is to me. It's not about having your face in the paper or having your name in lights or being seen at the right parties. It's about doing what you love doing and making a living out of it. I'll always remember great times, but my happiest memory ever in the business was when the Dublin poet, Pat Ingoldsby, introduced me to a packed house in the Olympia Theatre in Dublin. That was a big moment for me, to discover that I could command a crowd like that. It was the best gig I ever did.

Virtually all of my own songs are autobiographical and have been inspired by the real things, good and bad, that have happened to me over the years. I'm certainly not into writing empty 'I love you and you love me' type of songs just to get into the charts.

When I write I try to come up with songs with healing properties in them. I'm trying to get people to become more aware of themselves and the world around them and the lives they lead. Or I might write a song to help people grieve or to deal with a problem they might be struggling with. There has to be some serious purpose to the songs I write, otherwise I wouldn't see the point."

24

DONAL LUNNY

Donal Lunny has been at the cutting edge of the development of Irish traditional music for almost thirty years and is generally regarded by musicians and those who commentate on the internal affairs of Irish music as having been central to the resurgence in interest in traditional music over the past forty years. Each of Lunny's seminal groups (Planxty, The Bothy Band and Moving Hearts) has successively redefined the current state of the art in Irish music and attracted new fans to the genre from around the globe.

❝ My most vivid childhood memory of music is of standing outside my grandmother's house in Ranafast in Donegal at sunset on a warm, still summer's evening, listening to the faraway sound of an air being played on a tin whistle, clear and even, and in magical harmony with the mood of the dusk. At that moment I was enchanted by music. I was about seven years old. I have an earlier memory of a Christmas morning aged four, tiptoeing downstairs with my sisters and brother, and Máire, the eldest, was humming "walking my baby back home". Our mother hunted us back to bed (with our presents) because it was 4.30 am! But every time I hear that melody, that moment is vividly evoked: I'm back on the stairs, full of the most joyful anticipation, knowing that Santa has come.

Then there's the store of lullabies and songs which my father sang as he bounced us on his knee. Some of them had a surprise moment for which his knee would suddenly be gone, and he'd catch us before we landed on the floor. It worked every time. One of the songs he sang for us started :

Ould John McGee was as full as an egg,
He fell in the corner and broke his wooden leg . . .

And another one went:
She's my sweetheart, I'm her beau,
She's my Annie, I'm her Joe.
We'll get married, never more to part,
And little Annie Rooney is my sweetheart.

All my sisters and brother had these songs sung to them, so they pervaded our early years. But for many years I was unconscious of my parents' influence on my musical heart. My mother knew many songs in Irish from her own childhood, and often sang them to us. My childhood summers were spent with the family in Ranafast. There we spent up to eight weeks of the summer by the sea, speaking Irish, away from radios and tvs - in a very different world. I heard quite a bit of music and song while I was there. So by osmosis I grew to love the atmosphere and character of Irish music.

When I started arranging and performing traditional songs and music I was able to draw on the store of unconscious information I had accumulated over the years.

As far back as I can remember there was a piano in our living room. My three sisters, my brother and I all received piano lessons from Mrs Hangelaid, the wife of a work colleague of my father's and an excellent pianist from Estonia. I was five years old, and had a concentration span of about four seconds! So Mrs Hangelaid suffered great frustration with me, and frequently became exasperated.

As a result I came to dread piano lessons. One afternoon, I feigned sickness and solemnly went to bed to avoid having to face the music (literally!). My parents realised how desperate I was - normally they had great difficulty getting me to bed - and allowed me to stop. Nevertheless, in those six months of lessons I picked up a fundamental understanding of harmonic structure and metre, and it has stood to me ever since. Three of my sisters continued piano lessons, and when I was about twelve I became interested again in the piano. I began learning my sisters' piano pieces by ear, and would rattle them off just to confound them!

I can still remember the warm sound of the radio in the kitchen - and the smell of the hot valves through the perforated board at the back of the radio. Radio Éireann, as it was then called, broadcast performances of classical music which my father listened to. He loved the great composers, particularly Sibelius, and could identify the authors of most pieces from the style of the composition. I found this fascinating, though I didn't go out of my way to listen to his chosen programmes.

There was another exciting and romantic world: whenever my parents left the kitchen one or other of my older siblings would immediately tune in Radio Luxembourg. This channel was enormously popular, and broadcast the birth and rise of rock 'n' roll across Europe. Even though it consisted of wall-to-wall sponsored programmes (such as Horace Bachelor's 'Infra-

Draw Method' or H Samuel and his 'Ever-Rite' watch), the commerciality wasn't as ruthless as it has become in more recent years, i.e. there was room for a bit of taste here and there.

The first single I bought was 'Stardust', a bossa nova rendition by Ella Fitzgerald of which I couldn't get enough. Soon after that I heard Stan Getz and Charlie Byrd, and got their album. Pianist Dave Brubeck was next, and I got his 1961 album, *Time Further Out*, with the immortal 'Take Five' on it, along with 'Raggy Waltz' and 'Unsquare Dance'. Also during this period I started my secondary education in Newbridge College. Unfortunately I got off on the wrong foot, and my life was a misery until I left. Thankfully my father transferred me to a new secondary school started by the Patrician Brothers. The next three years were the happiest of my schooldays, mainly because we were all treated fairly.

Brother Maurice had an enormous collection of opera recordings, and during science practicals he would play something from *La Traviata* or *Il Trovatore*, quite loud, on his good record player. It was a lovely way to lighten the atmosphere. I'm sure many of my schoolmates developed a love for this music during their time there.

I joined my first band during this time. One of my classmates, Joey O'Shea, played an electric guitar, and suggested starting a rock band. There were many eager candidates, but eventually the potential trombonists and clarinet players dropped away; Mick Casey got a bass, Andy Moroney an electric guitar, I got hold of a broken-down kit of drums whose previous life was probably in a céilidh band, and the Cyclones were born! We did covers of The Shadows, and songs in the charts at the time. Tennis hops were about the limit of our gigging, but it was an exhilarating time. During furious rehearsals in a garage I started trying to play the guitar. But I was left-handed, and didn't get anywhere until I hit on the idea of reversing the strings (I thought I'd invented the left-handed guitar!). From then on my fate was sealed. I was nothing short of obsessed.

My first opportunity to play guitar publicly was with a ballad group called the Liffeysiders (Sean Reilly, Brendan Hayes, Justin Brady and Mick Curran). This was a magical time; it seemed the whole country was enchanted by the old traditional songs revived by the Clancy Brothers, and later, the Dubliners, and the huge number of ballad groups all over the country. We played a candlelight session every Saturday night in the Derby House Hotel in Kildare town.

My memory of the actual performances is hazy, but I can recall the pure pleasure of having the audience join in with us on the popular ballads we played. Christy Moore, whom I had known from the age of ten, was playing the guitar by this time, and for a short while we had a group called The Rakes of Kildare, which included my brother Frank playing whistle.

I hadn't decided on a career before I did my Leaving Cert, but art had always been one of my best subjects, so it was logical that I decided to go to the National College of Art and Design. However, my involvement in music escalated after I arrived in Dublin. And, though music absorbed energy I would have otherwise put into art, I believe the two activities actually complemented each other.

During my time in NCAD, I was part of a professional trio (Emmet Spiceland) and keeping up with my studies became a struggle. After I finished in NCAD, I made silver and gold jewellery in a workshop I shared with my classmate, sculptor Vincent Browne. At this stage I was doing various things musically: playing with the folk ensemble We 4; studio session work, music for tv films, and gigs with Andy Irvine. We had a weekly session in Slattery's in Capel Street in Dublin, called "the Mug's Gig". But I think at the time, my 'official' occupation was silversmith, and music didn't seem like a viable alternative.

During my silverwork period, Christy Moore came back from the UK where he'd been playing folk clubs for the previous five years. He recruited a clatter of musicians, Andy Irvine and myself among them, and we recorded the album, *Prosperous*, over a very enjoyable few days. Also involved in that session was Liam O'Flynn, and several months later Christy suggested we form a group, whereupon Planxty was born.

Our repertoire came together very quickly, and before I knew it, I hadn't time for the workshop. Almost overnight I became a professional musician. Although we had many crazily hilarious times together, we took our music very seriously. Liam was conscious of his integrity as a piper, and arranging the tunes and airs he played proved to be a great discipline for us. This attitude transferred naturally to the songs Christy and Andy chose, and we developed a strong sense of what was appropriate for tunes and songs, some of which were centuries old. This combination of songs and traditional tunes was a new thing, and gave the band wide appeal. Planxty was the first band of its kind, and a major turning-point for me.

I feel very lucky to have been involved with such great musicians in all the bands I've been part of, including Planxty, the Bothy Band, Moving Hearts, and most recently, Coolfin. For me, there was a progression from one to the next. Sometimes people ask me which band do I think was best, but there were qualities I loved in the music of each. The instrumental music of Planxty had an almost sonorous quality, because Liam more often than not chose to play reels and jigs a shade slower than usual. This gave the tunes a stately character reminiscent of a ship in full sail on the ocean. In contrast, the Bothy Band's music was fast and wild, and barely under control. In full flight it had more sheer animal energy than any other band I played with.

But it's difficult to identify any single moment as being 'the greatest'; I've always felt that, whatever point I'm at right now, there's more and maybe better to come."

25

D'SIDE

For many young music fans, D-SIDE is unquestionably one of the hottest new pop acts to emerge from Ireland. The line-up consists of Derek Ryan, Damien Bowe, Dane Guiden, Derek Moran and Shane Creevey. in 2002 they were the deserved recipients of the *Smash Hits* magazine "Best Newcomers' Award", a sure sign of their potential, since previous winners of the same award include Boyzone and Westlife. D-SIDE's debut single 'Stronger Together' was a hit in Ireland and in the UK and their fan-base has grown considerably during the current year.

DEREK RYAN

" I'm from Carlow, and I remember going to see my father play many times, even though I might have been only four or five at the time. He was in a band called Cupla. I remember dressing up the same as them whenever I went along to see them. My brother played the accordion and we all got into Irish music. Every Sunday morning after Mass we would all come home and have an informal session in our living room. I have really happy memories of all this and of travelling all around the country to fleadh ceols every year. It was just brilliant.

I remember the first gig I ever went to was Garth Brooks in Croke Park. So I started off with the best-ever concert I ever went to! Nothing so far has been better than that first gig. It was unbelievable, and had a huge influence on me. There were no amazing effects like you get at some gigs. It was all about the music. I thought it was amazing that one guy could get up on stage, sing with just his guitar and hold 70,000 people in the palm of his hand.

Being part of D'SIDE has been brilliant. Performing on the *Smash Hits* Poll Winners' Party and winning the "Best Newcomers' Award" was a very exciting experience. That would be the highlight for me so far."

FAVOURITE SONG: 'Summer of '69' by Bryan Adams

BIGGEST INFLUENCE: My father was a massive influence on getting us into music in the first place.

DAMIEN BOWE

"My most vivid memory of music from when I was much younger is of the first time I went to Ceoltas when I was about five years of age. It's like your first day at school, you're just taken there and you don't know what you're doing there, but you get into it. My parents took me along because I was always singing or dancing around the place when I was a kid. I'm from Straboe in County Laois, and the music my parents listened to was a big influence on me. They would have country music and Irish traditional music on when we were driving anywhere in the car. But the funny thing is that neither of my parents plays an instrument and they don't come from musical backgrounds. Sure my Dad can't even dance! He has no sense of rhythm! But all of my generation, my cousins for example, all did music and all learned Irish dancing.

The radio was a strong influence as well, as every Irish kid listens to the radio. When I was younger, Atlantic 252 was the big station for kids like me, but the station's gone now. Before I decided I wanted to go full-time in the music business, I would have loved to be a teacher. But I didn't have the brains for it (unfortunately!?!). Maybe if I had quietened down at school from an earlier age I would have been fine. I used to teach set dancing to lots of kids, and I used to love teaching it.

The best moment for me so far in the music business was when the band was promoting our debut single across the country. We went back to my hometown and had scheduled a promotional appearance at the Portlaoise Shopping Centre. While I was waiting in my uncle's house beforehand, somebody phoned to tell me there were a lot of people already waiting for us. When I got down there with the rest of the band there were 1,500 people waiting for us. I was so proud. That was the most amazing feeling. It made the hairs stand on the back on my hands."

FAVOURITE SONG: 'One Moment in Time' by Diana Ross

DANE (DAMIEN) GUIDEN

// When I was growing up I was a huge fan of both Boy George and Michael Jackson. I used to have this cardigan that I used to wear on my head, pretending it was long hair because I wanted to be like my heroes. I had a keyboard and I used to walk around everywhere with it while wearing my pretend wig. It was one of those small Casio keyboards that had little demo songs on it. I would press the demo song and pretend that I was playing it! It was a piano version of a Wham song; I'll never forget that. When anyone came into the house I would make him or her listen to whatever I could play. I wasn't even good at it, but I was a total show-off. My mother was so supportive. She saw I was really interested in music and bought me tapes to encourage me.

I'm from Coolock in north Dublin and I've always wanted to be in the music business. Thinking of it took me into my own little world. Before I got into the band I was wondering if it was ever going to happen for me, so I applied to do a Music, Production and Management course because I wanted to be involved in the music industry in some way or other. So when I got into the band it was like a dream come true."

SHANE CREEVEY

// My earliest memory of music is listening to vinyl records in the family house. My dad used to play a Stevie Wonder album and his hit song 'I Just Called To Say I Love You' all the time. Seeing Boyzone on the telly when they started had a big effect on me too. For everyone in a boy band that was a big memory. Those are the things that made me want to be a singer. I went to the Billy Barry stage school and never, ever wanted to do anything else. I've always wanted to be in a band, to make great music and perform for people. Being in this band is a fantastic experience. We have all put so much work into it and it has paid off. I have had some great times and I am very lucky.

My mam and my dad have always been a huge influence on me. From a young age my mam was the one who got me involved in the stage school and that helped start me off. They've always supported me and always told me that if you want something hard enough, you can get it."

DEREK MORAN

❝Thinking back, my earliest memory of music goes back to when I was doing a school play and my mother came along to see me in it. My family is a very musical family. My two sisters are dancers, and my brother is a really good singer, but I think it was my mam's mam who had the biggest influence on me. I used to go over to her place a lot just to play her records. She got me into it. I was a Billy Barry kid and I just did nothing else. All my life I've been in shows and pantos. That's how I was making my money and D-SIDE was the next step towards doing something else, so I never had any time to consider following any other career.

The first-ever concert I went to was to see Kylie Minogue and Jason Donovan. I hadn't actually planned to go to it. But my next-door neighbour, who used to baby-sit me, got tickets, so I went along. I was about ten and when you see a concert like that you kind of say to yourself that you want to be up there yourself some day."

26

ELEANOR McEVOY

Dubliner Eleanor McEvoy first came to public notice in 1992 as the composer of the hit duet with Mary Black, 'A Woman's Heart', which formed the lead track on a compilation album that went on to sell well in excess of half-a-million copies. Since then Eleanor has recorded four solo albums, including the latest *Yola*, on her own record label, and extensively toured Europe and the USA. Prior to emerging as a solo artist, she had been a violinist with the National Symphony Orchestra, played with Mary Black's backing band and accompanied Phil Coulter on a tour of the USA.

*"*Apart from a brief period when I wanted to be an astronaut, I've wanted to be a musician from as far back as I can remember. To quote a line from one of my songs, music to me is as 'potent as wine'. When I was only four I began to doodle with the piano in our home in Cabra in Dublin. I was encouraged by lessons I got from my sister

Marion. But then I saw somebody on telly playing a saxophone, so I wanted to play that instead and hoped to get one from Santa. But my mother felt that playing the sax was not something a respectable young Catholic girl did, and when Santa arrived my present turned out to be a violin instead. Thus began my turbulent relationship with the violin. I once even threw it across a room in a fit of temper.

Meanwhile my sister decided I should have piano lessons from a teacher, but the teacher also reckoned that, as I had a keen ear, I should learn to play the violin properly. So off to violin lessons I went as a strong-willed eight-year-old trying to unlearn all the bad habits I'd picked up on the instrument. But I made good progress, and in my late teens I had become good enough to play in small orchestras and in the National Youth Orchestra.

I went to Trinity College to study for a degree in music with a bunch of students who were all as fanatical about music as I was. Being a fairly broke student I gave violin lessons in the evenings to generate some welcome income. I did a bit of busking too, and played with pit orchestras for musicals such as *Oklahoma*. I accompanied artists as diverse as the Dublin rock band The Pale, and joined Phil Coulter for an American tour. In fact I eventually earned enough money to buy myself that saxophone!

I spent three great years with the National Symphony Orchestra. I found it a truly exhilarating experience, to sit in the middle of an orchestra playing a symphony by Mahler or Beethoven. But eventually I had to admit that I didn't love it enough to make it a life-time commitment and I left to travel the world with Mary Black's band. But I was also beginning to harbour ambitions to have my own band and to write my own songs. I wrote 'A Woman's Heart' during a period of depression and its success opened lots of doors for me, including record deals with two of the biggest companies in the world, Geffen and Sony, and enabled me to gather the confidence to start my own label later on.

Most of my songs are at least partly autobiographical, although it would be wrong to read something personal into every line. But there's something daunting, and at the same time therapeutic, about laying your innermost feelings bare for the whole world to see. I can also appreciate that sometimes people close to me, like my parents or close friends, might have difficulty with some aspects of the lyrics in my songs. But I have to write from reality rather than fantasy.

The music industry is a tough business to make a living from over a long period of time. Not only is there a heavy preference for youth, but it's still a very male-dominated industry and I find the sexism I meet hard to take at times. It's often happened that I've turned up to do a gig and the sound guy will direct me to my place behind a mike on the assumption that, being a woman, I must be a backing singer. It seems to be taking some of them quite a while to work out the fact that a woman might actually know how to play a proper instrument!

I don't have a regular schedule for writing songs. Over the past year I did tours of Britain, Ireland and the USA as well as having my first baby, Sarah Jane. I also recorded, released and did the promotional work for my album, *Yola*. There's little time in that kind of hectic schedule for writing songs, so I normally plan to set aside a specific period in which to write new material in my home near Tagoat in County Wexford. In fact the area I now live in inspired the title of that album.

I write the songs from my head onto sheet music in music notation. Unlike many songwriters, I don't use an instrument with which to compose the songs. When I have enough songs ready I usually get together with my keyboard player, Brian Connor, who also plays with me live. He's an invaluable sounding board and I respect his reactions to the songs and the musical ideas I might have for them. We knock the songs into shape and then pick the dozen or so which we want to record. Despite the occasional difficulties that beset all artists in what is a very competitive and very fickle industry, I feel genuinely privileged that I can make a career out of playing and recording my own music. In fact I can't imagine myself doing anything else.

Although both my parents were keen music fans they never had the opportunities I had to make a living from it in the way I and my brother Kieran and my sister Marion have done. But I'll always be grateful to my parents for encouraging me to play music in the first place."

FAVOURITE SONG: 'Music Shall Melt Away My Troubles' by Henry Purcell.

FAVOURITE SONGWRITER: It's hard for me to choose between Leonard Cohen and Bob Dylan.

FAVOURITE ALBUM: *A Love Supreme* by John Coltrane.

FAVOURITE ARTIST: Currently it's Natalie Merchant.

27

ELEANOR
SHANLEY

The legendary band De Danann, so impressed by her warm vocal delivery, first discovered singer Eleanor Shanley and they quickly appointed her their lead singer, a much-coveted position previously held by Mary Black, Maura O'Connell and Dolores Keane. Originally from Keshcarrigan in County Leitrim, for five years Eleanor toured with the band extensively around the world before, after careful consideration and planning, setting out as a solo artist in 1993. In 1995 she recorded her debut album, simply called *Eleanor Shanley*, an impressive work that in due course proceeded to achieve sales of gold status. As a solo artist she hasalready toured to great acclaim through numerous countries and played at countless high-profile festivals, but she has also shared stages with such established acts as Christy Moore, Ronnie Drew and Mike Hanrahan.

" Soon after I started school a teacher taught me a song called 'My Own Leitrim Home'. When I arrived home I started singing it for my mother and she said, "My God,

you have a great voice." All her sisters were singers, so they taught me a few songs and shortly afterwards I competed in the Tostal event in Drumshanbo in County Leitrim where I won first prize.

From then on, probably from when I was around seven or eight years old, my mother and family hauled me around from *feis ceol* to *fleadh ceol* to sing. It was great to see all the people up on the stage singing, but it was also very nerve-racking for me at the same time. You're there on the stage performing for people in front of a professional adjudicator who might sometimes be nice about your performance. But sometimes he or she might not be so nice and they might criticise you too! So that was a strengthening exercise for me as well, and the competitions were a great way for me to learn songs, to hear new songs being sung and to study other singers. It was a great education.

My mother has been one of the biggest influences on my music career, the one who would have been the most encouraging over the years. But both of my parents were very much on my side through my entire singing career, even in the later years. So even today they are a great influence on me. Gosh, when I think of them driving me around to fleadhs and all sorts of events and having to sit and listen to this stuff all day long, I don't know how they found the energy and the patience. If I had a child myself I don't know if I could do it.

While I was growing up I remember going to a career guidance teacher and telling her that I wanted to be a Bean Garda. Her reply was "That's no job for a woman!" But apart from that I've always wanted to sing, although I never thought it was going to be anything but an unfulfilled dream. I never thought it would become reality.

So I did all the usual things. I did the nine-to-five routines in Dublin, including working in FÁS for a few years in Baggot

Street. I even studied drama at night-time and at that stage I thought that if I were going to do anything artistic it would probably be acting. But a friend of Frankie Gavin heard me singing at a session in The Merchant, a pub along the quays in Dublin, so it was Frank Cooney and Ned O'Shea who introduced me to De Danann. It took me about three minutes to make up my mind and say "Yes" and take my place in one of the top groups ever to come out of Ireland.

I spent five years with De Dannan, making two albums with them, *Jacket of Batteries* and *Half Set in Harlem*. Then I made my first album, which was called *Eleanor Shanley* followed by the *Desert Heart* album. Following that I joined forces with Ronnie Drew, spending about a year and half touring with him. You could say I was working with my hero. Working with Ronnie was as exciting a step as joining De Dannan. Ronnie is the father of Irish folk and ballads as far as I'm concerned. We get on very well and we always have a great laugh together. It's a happy combination and I enjoy singing with him.

I have never ever felt frustrated in this business. If I ever do get to feeling that way and things really get me down, I just remind myself that I could be back behind that desk working in FÁS. That was literally just working to get the money to pay my way at the end of the week. But I made my two best friendships from working there, so I'm grateful for that experience anyway. As far as job satisfaction goes, I love doing what I do. I simply love it."

FAVOURITE ALBUM AND SINGER:
Just about anything by Leonard Cohen. He has great wit, and I like his sense of humour.

28

FIFTH AVENUE

Fifth Avenue, a five-piece group from Dublin, is made up of Mark Walton, Beverley O'Sullivan, Terry Gaynor, Jessica Molloy and Danny Cummins. Following the impressive success in 2001 of 'Spanish Eyes' and 'Party All Night', Fifth Avenue returned with another single 'Sometimes When We Touch', originally an international hit for Dan Hill in the late seventies, and promptly entered the Irish charts at number 3. This year sees the release of their debut album.

DANNY CUMMINS

"My most vivid memory of music as a child would definitely have to be all the Motown and soul records my father used to play by artists like the Stylistics, Stevie Wonder, Diana Ross and The Temptations. I now love those records myself, but my early exposure to those great old records has also led me to appreciate music by artists like Babyface and Brian McKnight who are such strong songwriters today, and who

117

influence me when I'm writing tracks for Fifth Avenue. My favourite song and artist is 'The Day' by Babyface, and his album of the same name is another great favourite of mine. I am fascinated by the way he writes about life, not just his life but other people's experiences too. The song 'The Day' is about his son. The lyrics are so powerful and they really affect you. I believe that is so important about songs, the ability to reach people with your words, and that is exactly what he does."

JESSICA MOLLOY
"I definitely think that radio has a huge influence on everybody in Ireland and is probably one of the key elements in encouraging artists towards a musical career. I remember the radio was constantly on in our house, allowing us hear the new songs that were around. Thankfully, all the radio stations throughout Ireland got behind us for each of the single records we released, and that support played a big part in developing our fan base and boosting our record sales."

BEVERLEY O'SULLIVAN
"My mother isn't what you'd call an amazing singer, but ever since I can remember she was constantly involved in musicals, theatrical performances and any dance classes she could get involved in. She also got me involved in the Billy Barry school as she herself used to be with that organisation as a child. She knew how much I would appreciate the experience, and I really did.

Between her and my father there was always music playing in our house. Artists like Sting, The Eagles and Fleetwood Mac were major favourites, and I completely loved them. The first gig I ever went to was Dina Carroll in the Point Depot in

Dublin. At the time she was a huge international artist and I was so nervous. I really didn't know what to expect from a concert, never having been to one. But it turned out to be one of the best concerts I have ever been to. She was so amazing and I was overwhelmed to see how many people were fascinated and touched by this woman's beautiful voice. And I remember coming home that night and telling my parents that one day I would be up there, on-stage performing my own songs.

Eight years later that promise came true when Fifth Avenue performed for the first time in the Odyssey Arena in Belfast and then at the Point Depot, supporting Westlife during their tour. It was an experience that is just so hard for me to describe. We had worked together for two years writing our own tracks and constantly rehearsing and dreaming about people hearing our music, and finally they did. We performed three of our own tracks and also got signed to RGB Records on one of those nights, so you could say our first gig together turned out to be so much more important than we could ever have expected.

My favourite song and artist would definitely have to be 'My All' by Mariah Carey, and her album *Butterfly* is also brilliant. I am a huge fan of hers simply because her songwriting is completely amazing and she writes about truth and that also appeals to me. Her albums always focus on some real experience she has gone through. She is such a strong woman who always comes back and doesn't care what anyone thinks. She is definitely a huge influence on me."

TERRY GAYNOR

" As a young child I had a great love of both singing and football. I always knew that I would end up following one of those careers one day, but I never really sat down to think about it. When I was a semi-professional footballer for a team I played with in the Leinster Senior League, everybody around me was convinced I would one day become a professional footballer. But I chose my musical career instead. As a child I was also involved in several stage shows at school, which I guess pushed me more towards the musical area I am in now. I was always writing songs and entering talent competitions. I had such a strong passion for singing and writing, so when I joined Fifth Avenue and we signed our first record deal, I knew this was exactly where I wanted to be.

Picking the best moment in music so far for me would actually be a close call between two different events. The first was when we released our first single, 'Spanish Eyes', which we had written ourselves. It was such a phenomenal experience for us. We couldn't believe that our song was being played on radio across Ireland and that we were appearing on television.

The second choice for my favourite moment would be when we released that same single across Europe. Territories like France, Scandinavia, Germany and Italy were hearing Fifth Avenue's sound and we just couldn't believe it. Our years of hard work had truly paid off."

MARK WALTON
"When you've been in the music industry as long as I have, having been involved in two other bands before Fifth Avenue and taken so many knocks, it can become extremely frustrating. But I can never have enough of the industry now because I am involved in a band who write their own material and are vocally amazing. We have so far struggled for three years and we are now in a position where I could never turn away from it all."

29

FINBAR FUREY

Born into a highly musical family from Ballyfermot in Dublin, Finbar Furey has been a major presence on the Irish music scene for more than four decades. As the lead singer and uilleann piper for The Fureys, a group he shared with his brothers Eddie, Paul and George, he helped to guide the evolution of Ireland's traditional music and bring that musical heritage to wide and appreciative audiences all over the world. In 1981 The Fureys became one of the rare Irish folk acts to crack the UK chart, reaching the UK Top 20 with 'When You Were Sweet Sixteen'.

" There was always music in our house, and pipes and flutes. I wasn't allowed to touch them because I was too young, but I yearned for something that I could play myself. One day when I was four or five my mother sent me out for butter. I looked in the window of a hardware store where they had a Clarks whistle, one of the old ones with a wooden mouthpiece. So I went in, picked it up and started to blow into it. I really enjoyed blowing into it. So I bought it with

the butter money and didn't go home! My father found me in the corner of a field trying to play it. I thought there would be war when he got me home. But my father was very smart. He bought the butter out of his own pocket, brought it home to the mother and put me in a corner with the whistle.

That's as far back as I can remember anything connected with music. I had heard the whistle being played and I simply wanted to get into it myself. My old man was great. He explained the instrument to me and within a week I was able to play it. I loved the tone of it and the feel of my fingers going up and down. He taught me how to read and write music, made me write out tunes and make up tunes. By the time I was seven I was fairly accomplished on the whistle and the pipes, which I'd first picked up when I was about six. I was knocking the reels out of them so well that people were saying there must be something wrong with me!

I loved anything to do with the Irish tradition. From an early age it was bred into me and I won my first singing competition when I was at school. I sang like a girl, and the boys would laugh at my soprano voice singing an Irish song. I learned so much from home, and people like the great piper Felix Doran who came to our house a lot. The Clare piper Willie Clancy stayed in the house many a time. Sean Maguire the fiddle player was another regular visitor. The house was always full of these wonderful musicians. We had no television, but the radio would be turned on for Radio Eireann's programme *Take The Floor* presented by Dinjo. He played some great céili bands. It was special back in those days.

I never thought of taking up any other profession. Even as a very small kid I wanted to be involved in music. I played all the time with my old man and travelled the road with him. He would pick me up from school with the pipes and a fiddle and we would head off down to Clare or Sligo or some place. I loved his company. We'd have a great laugh, putting tunes together. When we weren't playing music we would walk beside a river or go fishing or sit down while he told me stories about his past. He was just wonderful.

We had great parents. My mother was a great singer from Kilfenora in Co. Clare. My oul fella was from Galway. Sure, where could we go wrong? I won All-Ireland championships and the world championships on the uilleann pipes. I was also the All-Ireland whistle-playing champion way back in the sixties and I think I won an international folk award back in 1966 as part of the group with my brothers. We got paid £375 for a couple of gigs which was a ferocious amount of money. A man's weekly wage back then was about £4. I thought, "This is better than a day job! This is what I want to do."

The most enjoyable aspects of what I do is arranging old music and creating new music and songs. I still get a great buzz out of it. But I believe that either you write a song in ten minutes or you don't write one at all. My oul man had a great saying when we were kids:"If you can't feel it, leave it alone". In other words, if you don't feel like doing it well, don't do it at all. Never half do it.

I remember when I wrote 'Connemara Dawning'. I'd had a round of golf in Mayo with the Irish painter Frank Clark who does the *Simply Painting* programme on television. We headed to Clifden for a few pints and I had the pipes with me as always. Of course a session started up and before we knew it was morning. On our way home Frank and myself stopped to watch the sun rise. We sat down on this old Famine pathway, where the stones had probably been polished and worn by the bare feet of the poor people over centuries. We both felt very moved and I wrote 'Connemara Dawning' from that moment. It's about who we are and where we stem from. When I sing it on stage people just stand up when I'm finished because it means as much to them as it means to me.

I love discussing ideas with fellow musicians like Phil Coulter and Don Baker. It's something I miss since we did the *Four For The Road* tour, being on the road with very handy songwriters and creators like Don, Jimmy MacCarthy, Mick Hanly and Jimmy Faulkner. It was wonderful.

There's not a day goes by that I don't sit down with a piece of paper and a pen and write a song. I'll be happy as long as I can keep creating music that means so much to everybody. It's a great feeling when people are willing to pay to listen to you. I think it's only right to give at least 90 per cent of your heart back to them."

30

THE
4 OF US

Brendan Murphy

As a key member of the highly successful The 4 Of Us, Brendan Murphy's musical career spans more than ten years and four critically acclaimed albums – *Songs For The Tempted* (1989), *Man Alive* (1993), *Classified Personal* (1999) and *Heaven and Earth* (2003). Born in Newry, Co Down, Brendan and his brother Declan became what was to be the songwriting nucleus of a band that magically combined pop appeal with supremely crafted songs. One of those songs, 'Mary', has become one of the most played songs on Irish radio and the band are one of the most impressive acts on Ireland's live music scene, with a new album out in 2003.

"When I was on the college treadmill studying law at Queen's University in Belfast, I discovered that law didn't really interest me as a full-time profession. So I thought I'd prefer to do something I loved and my two biggest interests were music and film. So I worked it out that, if I were involved with music, then I could work at videos as well, so I would have the best of both worlds. I was a bit embarrassed about saying to anybody that I wanted to be seriously involved in music, so when it came to forming the band itself I suggested we keep it as a bit of a hobby. So we busked in France and got some money together and invested in a 4-track portable recording studio. We made up our own songs, which allowed us to create our own wee world as opposed to going out and embarrassing ourselves.

We were influenced by bands like Talking Heads and stuff where the instruments didn't sound like themselves but had been treated in a creative way to make fresh sounds. Wherever there were obviously odd things going on, that's what interested us. So we started recording demos and making our own videos, sent them off to record companies and it went off from there.

The great thing back then was that there was no pressure because I hadn't told anybody that we were doing this. The first anybody knew we were in a band was when we were offered a record deal. I thought that this was a bonus, writing songs, writing stories, basically writing your own script, doing the video and getting to act in it. I really enjoy being creative, it's as simple as that, looking into every possible scenario. It was that which interested me most, working on something worth creating.

When writing songs, it isn't interesting enough for me to write purely from fact. Whenever I'm trying to be creative I like looking into other people's lives or reflecting on my perception of someone else's life or a situation that someone went through. The whole point for me is to be able to escape the confines of my own life. That's the attraction of writing songs; you actually get to go into another world in your head and write a story about it.

The strange thing about music is that it has an emotional effect depending on the way you use instruments and the way people perceive it. It intrigues me that once you put music to your words it can really alter how you see that story. There have been lots of times when I've realised that this is the reason I do what I do. Then again, there have been a lot of times when I wonder why I do it! But it's really when you finish writing a song and you hear it, you get that magic feeling. When you walk into a record shop and you see your CD on the shelf, you get that feeling. When you hear a song you wrote two years ago on the radio, you get that feeling. It's like a photograph that you took that's in everybody's collection. It's a private process that has a public side to it. That's part of it. The risks and the odds are increased. I like that, and I love the way you have to redefine yourself constantly. I'd be bored doing the same thing over and over again.

Bob Dylan was a big influence on me. There were whole stories, and such freedom in the way he expressed himself. I loved Prince, so different and so original. You looked at this wee guy who came out with the sexiest songs in that decade. He made everyone else look ordinary. There are artists who have that emotional impact on you and it makes you want to go further, and I get that every year.

Music is such a fast-moving world that it's fun to be part of it. It's constantly changing and there's so much out there and if you wade through it there's so much amazing stuff. I still really like the music that I really liked when I was young. When the first Clash album came out in 1977 I remember buying it because I liked the cover. The guys on the front of it suggested in my mind that, if you walked down the wrong street, they would be looking at you. It looked rebellious and dangerous; it just exemplified freedom.

When you're younger, you sort of gravitate towards anything that has a big freedom sign above it. So much in your life suggests that, if you don't jump off the conveyer belt, you'll only end up doing what other people expect of you. At some point everybody has to decide where they want to get off, *if* they want to get off. Whether you find your interest is law or music, you have to make a choice at some point and maybe say, "This is where I get off."

Whenever I'd hear a really great album, say when I was about thirteen; that was when I first felt I might want to get off. But I didn't have the guts to get off the conveyer belt until I was living a double life as a student. That's when I said, "I'm going to have a go at it."

But if I got bored with all of it tomorrow I would give it up; it's as simple as that. You get one crack at it and the whole trick is to fulfil yourself and have as much fun as possible. That's what music is about for me."

31

THE FRAMES

Glen Hansard, lead vocalist

Glen Hansard is the charismatic lead vocalist with the chart-topping Irish band The Frames. With five superb albums to date, The Frames have built a huge fan base across Ireland and Europe and earned a reputation as one of the most entertaining live acts currently on the scene. Hansard's ability to craft heartfelt and thought-provoking lyrics is reflected in the acclaim that has greeted hugely successful songs such as 'Revelate' and 'Lay Me Down'. Nor has his acting ability gone unnoticed either, as Glen once starred in *The Commitments*, Alan Parker's internationally successful film that followed the fortunes of a fledgling working-class Dublin soul band.

"I remember an uncle, who died when I was about three, playing harmonica. I have this memory of being in a cot and looking through the bars and seeing him, his eyes looking really strange as his really thick glasses magnified them. That's my earliest memory of music, just hearing that harmonica. My uncle Paul played guitar. He had a really nice guitar and he would come and play in our house for my parents because all of my family was musical to some extent. He left a guitar for my big brother who expressed an interest in learning the instrument. But my brother never really picked it up. I remember it just lying on the floor. I don't know whether I was yet able to walk or not, but I lay on the floor pulling the strings, fascinated by the tones and the magic that seemed to come out of whatever this "thing" was. I threw it around like a toy; I didn't understand the preciousness of it at all. But every time I picked it up, people would frown and shout, "Be careful!" So the guitar had a place of importance in our house.

I don't have one stand-out moment when I took a step towards a specific interest in music. It was a more gradual thing. When I was older, the same Uncle Paul sat me down in the bedroom and showed me the chords E and A. I vividly remember learning them, and that was the only guitar lesson I've ever had.

But perhaps the subconscious decision to become a musician came when I was lying on the floor in our living room in Ballymun one Sunday. My granddad was there and I was watching Bob Dylan's video for 'Subterranean Homesick Blues'. I might have been only five or six, but I just fell in love with it. When the video came on, the whole house was told to "shush", because my mother was such a big Dylan fan, and for those few minutes while the video was on we were all transfixed by this guy. I remember thinking "Jesus, that's deadly!" I never really went down the Elvis or Jim Morrison of The Doors route. For me it was more Leonard Cohen and Bob Dylan, because my mother was such a fan of that music when we were kids. I remember sitting in the kitchen sink where our mother would bathe us, with the old suitcase record player up on the counter beside us. My mother would put on 'Bird On A Wire' by Leonard Cohen. She taught me the lyrics of that song and she taught my brother the lyrics of 'The Sound of Silence' by Simon and Garfunkel. We learned these songs so we could sing along with the records. Of course I didn't know what the lyrics of 'Bird On A Wire' meant until I was much older.

So the whole process of learning songs came to me very young. My mother used to hoover on a Sunday afternoon. I'd be there again lying on the floor listening to 'Jolene' by Dolly Parton and 'The Most Beautiful Girl' by Charlie Rich. Oh my God, I remember just loving that record! The noise of the hoover would be deafening anyway, but she'd have the record player cranked right up and all the windows open, the curtains blowing about and this amazing music blaring out of the stereo. These are great memories.

The first live music gig I ever attended was Christy Moore performing in a tent in Ballymun. He just came out to play. I don't even know what he was doing there. There was a tent pitched in the middle of a road and he played informally for a bunch of us. The first gig I ever paid into was The Police in Leixlip Castle. I went with my Uncle Paul who was a huge Police fan. I was blown away. I saw U2, who opened for them, and they were incredible. I was at the back of the field with my eyes fixed on those four little dots on stage. There was a great energy there that day. I came away from that gig going, "That band U2 are bleedin' brilliant!"

At that time the music I listened to was nearly all American, mixed with the folk stuff my mother was into. So I hadn't really got into music at all. But that gig kicked me off and I got heavily into AC/DC after that and went to see them in the RDS in Dublin. That was the first gig I attended on my own.

When I was a kid I wanted to be a fireman. I loved the idea of rescuing people from fires. Maybe that comes from the same want that being a musician comes from, in that I wanted to be a hero! (laughs) I never really planned being a musician. It just sort of happened that way. I got more and more into music and at the age of twelve became very introverted. Up to then I was doing all the things a young lad in Ballymun does at that age, drinking my head off, smoking and stealing things. I was heading down a bad road, getting into a lot of trouble at school. The police had knocked on my ma's door a few times. I don't know how it happened, but music was my saviour. Being so introverted, I got really into playing guitar, learning lots of Bob Dylan songs.

All I wanted to do then was go busking. I don't know why it was so important. There were no street musicians in my family; they were all balladeers that would play in the pubs. But I specifically wanted to go busking on the south side of Dublin. I'd never been on the south side. I remember a conversation with my form teacher in school. Frankie Byrne was my headmaster and he was also a DJ. When I was sent down to him he'd tick me off for whatever I'd done and say, "You're wasting your time. What are you at? You've a good brain, so why don't you use it?" and we'd end up talking about Bob Dylan. I was at the top of the school in terms of having a bit of intelligence, but I failed all my exams.

I went home one afternoon and told my ma that I had left school. She said, "If you're going to be lazing about this fucking house you better make some money!" So I went into town that day. I'd never been on Grafton Street before, my first time at fourteen years of age. When you're from the north side, you don't generally venture over because there was no real reason to, not back then anyway. I made 22 pence that day. Walking back home I stopped at the Mayfair Grill on O'Connell Street and bought myself a cup of tea. I've never drunk a cup of tea with more pride in my life. That my music had paid for that tea meant the world to me. It's been that way ever since, even when I went busking for two days in Prague. I eat after I busk with the money I've earned. I can't explain it, but it's the best feeling in the world.

I don't know what the future has in store for me. I've used an analogy before and it's the only way I can explain it. It's as if as a young lad I made a decision, a concrete decision. That decision sort of bought me a piece of land and I've been basically tending that land ever since. I strive to get better at what I do. I want to achieve, to improve and be a better songwriter."

32

FRANCES BLACK

Having begun her professional singing career in 1986, Frances Black has become one of Ireland best-known female voices. A former member of Arcady and The Black Family, 1993 saw her make her solo debut on the million-selling, all-female compilation, *A Woman's Heart*. Her first solo album, *Talk To Me*, was followed by three equally successful albums and extensive world tours, all culminating in the acclaimed release of her "Best of" album in 2000. In tandem with her musical partner Declan Sinnott, Frances continues to entertain audiences across the world and is featured heavily on various Irish music compilations including *Celtic Colours International Festival: Forgotten Roots*, the *Woman's Heart* compilations and *Loving Time*.

" My most vivid memory of music is the singing sessions that my mam and dad used to have in our house. Most Sunday evenings my dad would go to the local pub for a drink and he often brought a few people back to the house for a singsong .He somehow managed to bring the best out of people. Even people who were really shy, he would persuade them to sing. Another thing that stands out in my memory, even today, is of both my mam and dad laughing and being very happy whenever there was music involved. I think it was at this time that I learned that music could bring so much happiness to people.

My father came from Rathlin Island, a small island off the coast, and he had a traditional Irish music background. He played banjo, mandolin and accordion. My mother's background was a little different. She came from inner city Dublin and was an amazing singer. She sang all the songs popular in her time with the dance bands that entertained the public in Dublin. She was passionate about singing, so there was always music and singing in my house when I was younger. The radio was also a huge influence on my life as my mother was an avid radio listener, and it was switched on all the time in the house.

I think the first gig I ever went to was by Christy Moore, Donal Lunny and several other fine artists in The Meeting Place in Dorset Street in Dublin. It was a gig in support of the men in the H-Blocks who were at that time engaged in their "on the blanket" protest. The gig was intended to highlight their plight. My first gig as an artist was in Slattery's in Capel Street in Dublin. I had rehearsed for about a week with two excellent musicians. When the time came for me to perform I got up on stage and tried to sing. Unfortunately, nothing came out! I'd got a bout of stage fright and was so nervous I just totally clammed up and had to leave the stage in enormous embarrassment.

Given that kind of a start, I never ever dreamed that I would have a music career. When I was young my ambition had been to work with children. Sometimes I still have to pinch myself, because I consider myself so lucky to be in a career that is beyond my wildest dreams. I always loved singing, it was my passion, but I never really thought I was good enough to do it full-time. So it was a huge shock when my first album went to number one in the Irish charts and stayed there for ten weeks.

There are lots of great moments I can remember: It was really exciting when I won my first IRMA Award. But definitely the best moment for me was when I won my second IRMA Award. It was for the album, *The Smile On Your Face*. This was a really difficult time for me because I had completely lost my self-confidence and had damaged my vocal chords while doing a tour of the USA. It was a very dark time indeed for me and winning the award and realising that it was the people of Ireland who had voted for me gave me the strength I needed to carry on.

Yes, there have been many times when I felt I couldn't go on. Once again, the time that sticks out most for me was when I was recording the album, *The Smile On Your Face*. I just didn't feel strong enough because I had lost my confidence and again the thought that I'll never be good enough came in to my mind. But today, thank God, I'm not as hard on myself as I was then. I've come to the conclusion that even though I'll never be a technically brilliant singer of the calibre of someone like Celine Dion, I know how to put my heart, my soul and all the passion I have into the songs I pick. Those songs mean so much to me and are especially relevant to my life. I think people can relate to my songs, and that in itself gives me enormous pleasure.

FAVOURITE SONG:
My favourite song is 'Over The Rainbow' by Judy Garland because the words are amazing. The message I take from

this song is that no matter how dark life seems to be, there is always a glimmer of hope, like a rainbow, and life eventually gets better."

FAVOURITE ARTIST: James Taylor

FAVOURITE ALBUM: *Mud Slide Slim And The Blue Horizon* by James Taylor. This was the first album I ever owned. I got it as a present from my first boyfriend when I was 15. That album says it all for me.

33

GAVIN FRIDAY

Born in Dublin in 1959, Gavin Friday showed a keen interest in music from an early age. His first successful foray into the world of music was when he took the role of lead singer with one of Ireland's most ambitious and thought-provoking post-punk groups, the Virgin Prunes. The Prunes released several provocative albums in the early eighties before splitting up. The following decade saw Friday release four superb solo albums produced in tandem with his writing partner, Maurice Seezer. Having received much critical acclaim, the two have contributed to various film soundtracks, with credits including *Moulin Rouge, Romeo and Juliet* and *In the Name of the Father*. Gavin has also acted as a consultant to various musical projects in different art forms.

" I was the eldest child in our family, so I had no big brothers to be a bad influence on me. But, apart from trad sessions in our house with my da and his mates locked out of their heads singing Republican songs and anything else that came into their heads, my first memory of pop music was

T-Rex. They would have been the first band I got into, and that was when I was around twelve. It was a bit of everything that got me into their music, and when you're that age I guess you'll buy anything.

The first single I ever bought was called 'Popcorn' by Hot Butter, an instrumental lump of rubbish. When you're a teenager you want your own identity, and I think I was attracted by the fact that it was something new. There was a hippy thing with the Beatles going on around Ballymun, the suburb in Dublin where we lived, but I was too young for the Beatles. You were aware of them, but 'Popcorn' was fresh with a glam feel to it. It was just great pop music. It was Bolan, T-Rex, Roxy Music, all of that stuff. I thought I had a personal relationship with David Bowie and Marc Bolan because the music was so personal and because when you are younger you imagine you're the only one listening to that piece of music.

Thinking back, it was David Bowie who really blew my mind. He won me over and that was it. I became a total Bowie freak. It's obvious he was such a major influence on the Virgin Prunes, but more visually than musically. Glam has a bad reputation these days because everyone immediately thinks of bad hairdos and Slade. But check out Bowie, Roxy Music and the T-Rex records, and those pop singles still sound amazing today, thirty years later.

When I was around ten I wanted to be a priest or a Franciscan monk, but I doubt if they would have allowed me in! When you make your holy communion and your confirmation, you think God is talking especially to you. When the candles flicker as you are being confirmed, you think it's a special message. But I think being in the Virgin Prunes changed all that.

When I grew up thirty years ago the options were the dole, the Civil Service or the bank. The seventies were pretty rough economically, so you were being pushed more towards the dole. But my mates and the people I grew up with were also big influences. We were all the same age — Bono and Guggi, and we all helped each other along. Ballymun was a pretty rough place in those days, and we all fell in love with music and had a dislike for football. We all said that one day we would form a band.

I come from a Catholic background, but when I started hanging about with my mates and looking at the Protestant ethic, it was far more encouraging for me. I thought that Protestants had more confidence. Maybe they had more money too. When U2 started, their school gave them rehearsal rooms where they could make as much noise as they wanted. If your ear was pierced, that was grand. But we couldn't rehearse there because I didn't go to Mount Temple.

Those were the days when you didn't have much pocket money. You had to save up if you wanted something. To buy Bowie's *Ziggy Stardust* album was a fairly big expense. I had part-time jobs, including one with a turf accountant, and from that income I saved to buy my first stereo. My mates would swap records with each other, but because I had that part-time job I had more money than them.

When I was fifteen I used to get on the B&I boat and go over from Dublin to Liverpool just to buy records for me and my mates. I wasn't what you might call a 'Del Boy'. I wasn't doing it to make a few quid; it was to get the new Buzzcocks EP or whatever else seemed essential at the time. This was when the punk thing started kicking in and you couldn't get the albums over here, so I just went day shopping, hanging out in Probe Records.

Politically, punk gave us a licence to perform as a band because there was a great myth about music in those days. You used to think that you had to go to university and get a degree.

You would look at other geniuses and go to their gigs, but you couldn't actually form a band yourself. Punk broke that myth and said, "So what if you can't play guitar very well. Just get up and scream and express yourself." So I think that was the biggest kick and jolt I got. I thought, "I can actually do this."

The first gig I went to was the Arthur Phybes Band. I saw them in the Baggot Inn in Dublin and it was dreadful. But the first gig that blew my mind was The Radiators from Space in UCD in 1976 when I was about sixteen. I also saw Bowie in 1976 with his "Station-to-Station" tour. I got the train over, slept in the tube station, put on the eyeliner and went to see him at Earl's Court in London. It did my head in.

That was the gig that turned my head around. I was on my own, and felt a like a mucker compared to what London was about. It was the first time I ever saw real punks. There were loads of Bowie clones too, queuing up to get in, but there were all these people dressed up like post-holocaust Ziggy Stardust fans. I had long hair at the time, so when I got back home I cut it off, put in five earrings and I was away!

The first gig I played was in Sutton in north Dublin, and I had no other band members, apart from my friend Guggi. We were actually supporting U2. A week later we picked the rest of the band and The Virgin Prunes played their first gig in late '77 early '78 at the Project Arts Centre in Dublin. Two weeks later we supported the Clash in the Top Hat ballroom near Dun Laoghaire. We were bottled off stage and the Clash tossed us out because we were so lewd. But we didn't go out to entertain. In those days I was an angry young man and I took the punk ethic very seriously. It was teenage angst going full throttle."

FAVOURITE ALBUM: Patti Smith *Horses*

FAVOURITE SINGER: Billie Holiday.

34

THE HOTHOUSE FLOWERS

Fiachna O Braonáin, lead guitarist

Fiachna Ó Braonáin is the lead guitarist with Hothouse Flowers. Since being formed by Ó Braonáin and lead singer Liam Ó Maonlaí in the early eighties, the band has enjoyed enormous national and international acclaim. Originally formed as a street performance act, the band went full-time after winning a "Street Entertainers of the Year" award in 1985. Utilising an eclectic mix of traditional Irish music and rock, Hothouse Flowers created a distinctive sound, insisting on using the Irish forms of their individual names and even using both Irish and English in their song lyrics. Their album catalogue includes such gems as their 1988 debut, *People,* through to their recent top-selling *Best Of* release. Hit singles include 'Don't Go', regarded by many critics as one of the best Irish singles of all time, and their reinterpretation of the eighties hit, 'I Can See Clearly Now'. Individual band members have all enjoyed their own solo projects and collaborations.

" My earliest memory of music is probably a song by a folk-singer called Burl Ives. It went something like "If I had a little fishy, on a little dishy". I think the song was called 'When The Boat Comes In'. I was very young when that song was being played in the house, maybe only two or three at the time. It was definitely one of those songs that caught my imagination. There was a comical aspect to it in the way he sang it, his intonation. It made me laugh. My memory of it is fairly patchy now, but our memories can be reinforced a little by the way our parents tell stories later on.

We had a record player and both of my parents played piano. When I was about six or seven my dad took up playing the clarinet and I took to playing the recorder and soon after moved on to the tin whistle. I took to music straightaway, and I remember vividly the day my dad took me out to buy my own tin whistle. I was seven years old. I still remember it because the minute I got the whistle it just seemed I had a knack for it. I sat the whole day playing it and I was able to play a couple of tunes by the end of the first day. It was one of those days I will never forget, a pivotal moment, and I can still recall very clearly that it felt like something I really enjoyed. So fair play to my father for giving me such encouragement. He hung out with me all the time.

As I grew up I never really thought of what career to choose. Like all boys the thought of becoming a Guard might have had a passing fantasy appeal. During my early teens, career guidance teachers in school started implanting thoughts in all our minds, encouraging us to start thinking of what we might do when we left school. One of these surveys asked about things that you enjoyed doing, and my replies really revolved around music. I remember thinking that if my career guidance survey is rubber-stamping my decision to become a musician, then maybe it's not that unrealistic.

Yet despite that I went to university and studied law. I suppose I was going down the 'real job' road, although that didn't last too long. Within a year and a half in college the band was up and running. The university gave me two years' 'leave of absence' so I could come back and finish where I left off, which was unprecedented in UCD. It was a tough decision, but a necessary one for me. It was tougher for my parents to accept it. Even though I've had nothing but support from them all the way, I think it made them feel a bit better that I took 'leave of absence'. It probably eased some of the worries they had.

So much of life is about risk. You take risks every day. I'm very glad that my risk worked out. I think it's an incredibly privileged place to be, to be a working musician and to have a band that has lasted so long; it's like having another family really. To be able to get up and play in front of people and make a living out of that is wonderful.

Other things that influenced me when I was growing up were the radio. 2FM first coming on air was really an exciting time. It was the first Irish pop music station and we all had our 2FM 'cominatcha' stickers. Before that I listened to the pirate stations, like Radio Dublin and Radio Nova. I used to listen to the Big D first thing in the morning before I went to school. Before you ever started buying records, radio was where you heard your music.

I remember one stand-out moment of radio listening was when Madness played in Dublin for the very first time. I was only about 14 and I wasn't allowed to go out to gigs at the time. But the gig was broadcast on one of the pirate radio stations and I tuned in for it on medium wave. I think they broadcast it by literally lifting a phone from a coin box in the venue and holding it up for the whole gig! This is what went out on the radio, pure genius! That moment had such a mystery about it and held such a fascination for me. In one sense it was crap sounding, yet in another way it was so exciting for me as a fourteen year old, feeling the crowd and hearing the cheers and the music. I was a big fan of Madness and the Specials and all that ska music, so this was an amazing discovery for me.

I've had so many special moments through music. One of the few times I missed a gig was for the birth of my child twelve years ago. We played a gig in Cavan recently and I ran into people in Dublin who were at it and they say it was the most amazing gig that they had ever seen. So the great moments in my memory tend to be the most recent ones, although I tend to think the best moments lie ahead in the future, even though some people might perceive us as a band that had our heyday in the eighties.

But for me the 'heyday' is really only about to happen now. It's a good way to look at things. I don't really believe in nostalgia, and it's nice to have good memories, but it's important to be looking forward to the next record and the next tour.

There are a lot of people who were big influences for me. Obviously my parents supported and nurtured my interest in music and I'm eternally grateful for that. There were music teachers at school who were certainly influential. There was one guy, Micheál Ó hAluin, also known as Mick Allen. I think he still teaches music. He was my music teacher in secondary school and he was a big influence. When I was in first year the band in sixth year were my big heroes.

In our late teens we discovered black R'n'B and Soul music and they were huge influences on the Hothouse Flowers, especially in the mid-eighties when music had become a bit sanitised. We were then getting to hear the incredible and exciting music we hadn't heard when we were growing up, like Aretha Franklin and James Brown. The Rolling Stones (still big heroes of mine), BB King and early Rod Stewart also really influenced me.

FAVOURITE SONG: 'You Can't Always Get What You Want' by The Rolling Stones

FAVOURITE ALBUM: *Joy* by Isaac Hayes

FAVOURITE SINGER: Aretha Franklin

35

JACK L

Originally from Athy, Co Kildare, 29-year-old Jack Lukeman (otherwise known as Jack L) has earned the reputation as one of Ireland's most dynamic live performers. His voice has been described by one learned critic as 'a mixture of all the great male singing voices of the twentieth century'. Over the years he has been compared to Scott Walker, Frank Sinatra, Jim Morrison and Tom Waits, artists he generously admits to having been inspired by. His 1999 album, *Metropolis Blue*, has already achieved platinum status.

❝ My first vivid memory of music centres around a song we used to sing as kids that went "The bus ran over Mickey's head, doo, da, doo, da!" Please don't ask me where it came from. In fact I haven't heard it since my childhood, but it was a big hit on the Páirc Bríde estate in Athy in County Kildare when I was about four years old. Also from back then I can remember 'Two Little Boys' by Rolf Harris and the whole family listening to Abba on those big old tapes in the car when we went on holidays. The line "I dream I'm an eagle" from their song 'Eagle' is one that sticks in my mind after all the years. The radio was always on in our house as far back as I can remember. It would be on all day. I can remember hearing songs 'Rhinestone Cowboy' by Glen Campbell. I often think of that song nowadays because it has that line about "getting cards and letters from people I don't even know". That actually happens to me nowadays. Also, I can recall hearing Tom Waits' "The Piano Has Been Drinking" and it having a profound effect on me then. I'd never heard anything like that before. It would be fair to say that song and that voice had a big influence on me.

The gift of song always graced our house. My father has a fabulous voice. I remember my grandfather Jack Keogh listening to records by the Irish tenor John McCormack on Sundays. Several times as a kid I was woken up by late night singsongs in the house. Everybody had to play their part and sing a song or tell a story. My brothers and sisters were old enough to buy records, so I listened to whatever they brought home and played in the house. One of the first concerts I attended was when I went to see A-ha in Dublin when I was about thirteen or fourteen. I can't remember the concert itself too well, but I loved the band and recently went to see them again when they played The Point in Dublin. That was quite a nostalgic occasion.

When I was a young lad I wanted to be either a priest or an astronaut. I'd like to think I landed somewhere in between. But because I could always sing I have always been mesmerised by music. I remember singing "a-wop-bop-a-loo-bop-a lop-bam-boom" from 'Tutti Frutti' by Little Richard into a sweeping brush I pretended was a microphone, in my local youth club during a talent show. Over the years music developed from a passion into an obsession for me. It always seemed like a wild dream to actually do it as a profession, but somehow I managed to make it happen. When I was serving my time as an apprentice mechanic, I was often lying under cattle lorries, with cowshit dripping down on me, while I wondered how I was gonna escape and get into music. So eventually I just ran away and started busking around Europe, and that was that.

Other people might understandably assume that the best moments in my music career would be obvious things like playing The Point or achieving platinum sales figures for my records. But to me it's the continual learning and evolving and the fact that I am never totally fulfilled. There's always that next step to take. That's what drives any artist on. But every gig, every song you write, each song you record, each one seems like you're getting closer to that indefinable goal. Or further down the road towards something you can't quite explain. And there are countless moments of magic within the doing of all of these things.

I have never liked the music business. It's an unnatural marriage, an oxymoron. Music comes from a soulful, spiritual place. To put a number on it or manipulate it has always seemed wrong to me. But that's the age we live in. Most music contracts are a scam. In any other business they would be laughed at, but for some reason record companies get away with it. I also find it criminal that radio stations play what is essentially "bottom of the barrel" music, the lowest common denominator. I think it's an insult to people's intelligence to constantly play inoffensive sugary pop when the world is full of so many diverse musical talents.

I firmly believe that music can do more than make a quick buck for the capitalist dictatorship that is the corporate music industry. I think it has a greater value than that. It can heal people and comfort them. It can help us to evolve, expand our minds, help us to understand each other, to evolve ideas. It's the ultimate communication and one of the most ancient. But maybe that's just how I see it. I can't name a specific favourite artist or one album that stands out above all others. The myriad choices make it too hard to choose one. Every week whatever might be my then favourite changes to something else, and this is what continually fascinates me about music, its ever-changing, shape-shifting appeal."

FAVOURITE SONG:
John Lennon's 'Imagine' is often voted the greatest song of all time. And although I have a billion favourites I have to agree that it is. I love it for its all encompassing simplicity and the ideology it espouses.

36

JAMES GALWAY

James Galway is regarded as one of the greatest flute players in the world. His prodigious talent was obvious from an early age, winning all three classes of the Irish Flute Championships at the age of ten. 1969 saw him join the illustrious Berlin Philharmonic Orchestra, and five years later he launched his solo career with a recording contract with RCA Records. Since then he has gone from one major achievement to another, including a major international pop hit record with his instrumental version of John Denver's 'Annie's Song' in 1978. From multi-million selling albums to playing for countless dignitaries across the world, 'The Man With The Golden Flute' has won numerous honours and collaborated with many of the world's top artists.

My earliest memory of music would have been playing at school. When we went to the local park to play football I used to play the flute in front of all the kids, playing 'The Sash Me Father Wore' and all those Orange tunes I grew up with. It's amazing that the other children didn't make fun of me. But they would probably have got a belt from one of the teachers if they had! Then I made a big leap forward and began to play with the local drama societies, doing all sorts of things like Gilbert and Sullivan tunes and stuff by Bach and so on.

The radio was a big influence on me. To some extent it was the only influence, as we didn't have television in our house. We used to listen to David Curry and his *Irish Rhythms Show* in the morning. In the evening we would listen to Jimmy Shand's band as well as music by Henry Hall. Hall had a big band. It was fantastic, and they played great music.

Of course I also listened to the Proms when I got a bit older and more educated about music. We didn't have a television in our house until I'd started at the Royal College of Music in London in 1954 and came back one Christmas to find a tv had been installed. I think television is a great leveller. It brings everybody down to its own level, whereas if you listen to something, or somebody tells you a story on the radio, your imagination takes flight and you imagine all sorts of things. But your imagination doesn't go wild when something is presented to you in living colour. You can read a book and think it's great, but then you go to see the movie and you're disappointed. The movie is rarely anywhere near as good as your imagination.

My dad played the piano accordion and my mom played the piano. They had a trio going with a friend who played a violin. Eventually my brother joined in with them. He played the saxophone and clarinet. I never got into it, but they did have an influence on me. They didn't play dance music exclusively. My dad knew Mozart symphonies and other music like that, and I learned the themes from Mozart's *Jupiter* symphony from him. Eventually we took lessons, and when I was about twelve I started having formal flute lessons from a woman called

Muriel Dunne who was a student of Jeffrey Stewart who played with the Royal Philharmonic Orchestra.

I can't remember the first concert I ever went to, but I remember once my teacher or her husband saying there's a guy playing Chopin preludes tonight and we should go to it. So I rolled up there and I was listening to this guy playing all this stuff. Meanwhile my teacher's husband started to fall asleep and I didn't know what to do! Then he woke up and said, "God, is he still playing that stuff!" Some time later we got into a bus and went to Dublin to hear the opera, *Falstaff*. I was hooked, even though going to Dublin was more interesting than *Falstaff*. It was another example of your imagination running riot when you're young. I thought all those Catholics down there would have horns on their heads!

I didn't think at the start that music would be my career. As a matter of fact, when I was at school we learned bookbinding and I became quite good at it. I still know how to bind a book, but of course they don't do that any more; it's all done mechanically. But in those days they had to bind books and I tried to get a job doing that. Unfortunately, when I turned up looking like I did, bearing in mind the part of Belfast I was from, they probably thought I was looking for the orphanage! You have to understand what I used to look like. If you know Frank McCourt's book about Limerick, *Angela's Ashes*, well I looked like yer man in it, complete with black knees and all. So I didn't get the job, and it didn't stop me playing the flute.

Back then it was difficult to get jobs and I thought I was mad myself, giving so much time to the flute. In a way everybody could get a job, but some people were more particular about what they did. I wasn't too particular, and I got a job earning a few shillings a week in a piano factory. It wasn't the ideal job; I wanted to be the manager of the world's biggest band, but that particular vacancy wasn't available at the time, if you know what I mean! But then the government came to the rescue and made grants available to underprivileged children, and I won a scholarship to the Royal College of Music in London.

So it all came good in the end. You start chipping away at it, chiselling away at it every day. Every day brings a new thing. Something else happens afresh and you go along that road and try to make sure you stay on the straight path."

FAVOURITE SONG: This is a very difficult question. If I was on a desert island I would take an opera with me, one by Verdi or one by Puccini. Either way, it would have to have Joan Sutherland in it.

37

JERRY FISH
AND THE MUDBUG CLUB

Jerry Fish is the alter ego of singer Ger Whelan who through the late 80s and 90s was the main creative force in An Emotional Fish, the Irish rock band who released one of the most successful debut Irish albums ever. The band recorded two more albums in an action-packed career that also saw them supporting such class acts as Nirvana, Blondie and The Velvet Underground. After the band released their final album in 1995, Ger took some time away from the music business before reinventing himself with his band, Jerry Fish and the Mudbug Club. The debut solo album, *Be Yourself*, was released to critical acclaim in 2002, while a key track from the album, *True Friends*, was used prominently by mobile phone giants Vodaphone in a nationwide television campaign. Not surprisingly then, Jerry/Ger sealed a supremely successful comeback by winning an Irish Meteor Music Award.

"I have two musical memories that really stick out in my mind from when I was a youngster. The first is the sound-track music from the movie, *The Jungle Book*, of which I'm still a big fan. Later on, when I was about eight or nine, I would have moved on to Marc Bolan and T-Rex. It was their whole sound that really got me. It was a very simple sound that has lasted through the years and has influenced a lot of more modern top stars, including Prince. I grew up in London in the 70s, so from T-Rex I moved on to David Bowie, and listening to Bowie I got to learn of Lou Reed and the Velvet Underground and all that New York stuff. So one thing led to another, but if I were to pinpoint those earliest memories and influences they would have to be *The Jungle Book* and then T-Rex.

My father was a singer. He never sang professionally, but he often entered singing contests and regularly came home with bottles of champagne he had won. He collected records and had everything from Dean Martin to Pink Floyd in the house. He listened to Frank Sinatra and The Rolling Stones in particular. He had quite an eclectic taste and, in a way, I suppose that factor in turn had a big influence on me. Now I've kind of come full circle, because what he did back then is the sort of music that I'm performing now, known as crooning. I've always been a big fan of that style of singing, of which Sinatra is the all-time heavyweight champ.

From when I was a kid, singing was all I ever wanted to do, and I've never really had any other ambition. But I didn't really join a band until I was around seventeen. It came about after I answered an ad in *Hot Press* magazine. Some band was auditioning for a singer, so I answered the ad and away I went. The audition was the first time I had ever spoken into a microphone, let alone sung into one. It was very strange feeling really. I just fell into it. I had done a lot of travelling when I was younger, and after growing up in London I moved to

Dublin. I had never really settled down, so I suppose it was music and bands that got me to stay put.

The first gig I ever went to was a big influence on me. It was Thin Lizzy at Dalymount Park. It was a big summer festival; the Boomtown Rats were playing on the bill, as were the Radiators. It was also the first time I smelt marijuana! After that, Phil Lynott definitely became my idol. I actually followed him around on the band's 'Live and Dangerous' tour. I went to shows in Glasgow, Edinburgh and Dublin. I feel that the album of that tour, also called *Live and Dangerous*, is one of best live albums ever. So 'Philo' was a massive influence on me as a teenager. Because of him, the first instrument I ever picked up was the bass guitar. Herbie Flowers was also a big influence. He played the famous bass line on 'Walk on the Wild Side' by Lou Reed.

My own first gig as a public performer took place at the Baggot Inn in Dublin. I remember feeling very happy and comfortable on stage, so I really enjoyed it. A gang of mates came out to see us, but I can't even remember whom we supported. It might have been some local band like Katmandu. The Baggot was to be the place where we later met our record rep from Atlantic Records who signed us when I was with An Emotional Fish. So the Baggot, which I believe is being levelled at the moment, was for an awful lot of people, especially in Dublin, a very special music venue. It has well earned its place in Irish rock music history.

I've had quite a few ups and downs in the music scene. Touring with An Emotional Fish will always be something special to remember, but if I'm asked to pick one particular 'up' moment, I'd have to admit I'm really enjoying the Jerry Fish and the Mudbug Club thing at the moment. It has given me a new lease of life, and I feel more relaxed and freer with it. The biggest buzz I'm getting is from owning my own record label.

In a way it's an accumulation of all the experiences that I have had and the knowledge I've gained during the fifteen-odd years that I have been involved in the music scene. I really am enjoying that, just putting all I've learned to work for myself.

Right now is a really healthy time for Irish music with all the independent labels and that independent spirit. I think it encourages more creative stuff because you have nobody to answer to; you put it out there and it's the public that decides. It's far better than going through a filter of A and R departments and people who 'know better than you', or so they think. Previously, formulas had developed in music and that tended to stifle a lot of creativity. So it's great to see independent record companies doing their own thing and thriving with it."

38

JJ72

Mark Greaney, lead singer

Born in Dublin in 1980, Mark Greaney is the lead singer with three-piece Dublin-based band JJ72 who first formed in 1997. Their debut album has sold over 500,000 copies worldwide. With the support of drummer Fergal Matthews and bassist Hillary Woods, Greaney and JJ72 continue to thrill audiences at home and abroad with their dynamic live performances.

"There are many musical moments which mark my memory of being a child. But the one truly prominent memory is an amalgamation of pride and embarrassment. I was about nine years old and my father and uncle were in the sitting room of our house with the radio playing as they talked. 'Hot Legs' by Rod Stewart came on, and without further ado I took a sweeping brush in my hands (this, of course, was supposed to be my mike stand) and gave my first, and quite possibly best, performance before an audience. Don't ask why that moment had to be inspired by Rod Stewart!

My mother could play some chords on the guitar and piano and has a fine singing voice. My parents bought me a guitar and a violin when I was seven years old, so a noise that was supposed to be music could be heard in our house from about that age.

Top Of The Pops was on our television every week. For some reason it seemed to have a little bit more kudos back then than it does today. The Fine Young Cannibals, Pet Shop Boys, Bryan Adams and Transvision Vamp were all part of my musical intake. It remains to be seen whether that, especially Transvision Vamp, was a healthy thing for an impressionable young boy!

I think I was a late developer regarding gig-going. I remember seeing Aled Jones in concert, but I don't think that counts, as he's not very rock'n'roll. The Foo Fighters was the first real rock gig I went to and I still have very vivid memories of it. I think it was in late 1995 when they played in the SFX in Dublin. Most of my friends and I went, not because we knew the music of the Foo Fighters very well (that was irrelevant at the time), but because Dave Grohl had been the man behind those huge thunderous drums in Nirvana. The gig was louder than war and almost as violent, perfection for a fifteen-year-old with rock aspirations above his station.

The first gig I played was the following year in Eamon Doran's pub in Dublin's Temple Bar. It was a Saturday afternoon and JJ72 was the fifth band to go on stage out of what seemed like twenty. We, of course, were convinced that this was to be the most important twenty minutes of our lives. Every man and woman in the audience became a record company scout for a split second in our innocent eyes. We, naturally, learned many lessons from those twenty minutes. Number one lesson: it's always a good idea to be well rehearsed. Number two lesson: it also helps if you have actually written some lyrics for your songs! But there was some consolation in that we received ten pounds for our efforts.

When I was considering what I wanted to be, the thought of becoming a doctor appealed to me, until I realised needles are the work of the devil. I get dizzy even thinking of them. I never wanted to be a member of a police force or a scientist either.

I was brought to the National Concert Hall on a couple of occasions when I was young. As a result, an overwhelming desire to conduct an orchestra engulfed my soul for approximately one year. However, I don't think anyone appreciated my use of a carving knife as an improvised baton. But music was always calling in some form.

I would probably be expected to claim that there was a particular JJ72 gig which I would nominate as my best moment in music so far. But that would be lying, as I feel being in a band writing your own music is akin to chasing perfect happiness. It is unattainable. My best moment in music was actually while playing violin in an orchestra attempting the music of another being far greater than myself. I was sixteen and at a rehearsal preparing for a concert hall performance. I cannot remember the piece of music or the composer, but for one note in that rehearsal every instrument played in perfect unison. The result was spine-tingling beauty. Heaven was in that otherwise moribund classroom in Drumcondra for ten seconds. It was those ten seconds which still make me want to write music today.

Every third day I feel as if I have had enough of the music business. I don't think I could ever grow weary of music itself ... but of the business, yes I could. It contains so many people with so much to say about nothing.

FAVOURITE SONG: I always find it difficult to commit to going into print with my favourite song because, as with most of us, it changes on such a regular basis. But there is one song which can endure every mood of every day, 'Love Will Tear Us Apart' by Joy Division, an undoubted classic. It is possibly one of the greatest love songs ever written. From the tribal resonance of the opening drumbeat to the stoic mournfulness of the closing keyboard line, it's a perfect pop song."

FAVOURITE BANDS: Nirvana and the Smashing Pumpkins would have to be my two favourite bands simply because they represent the passion and pain of the infamous teen years. These two bands were the sonic foundations on which JJ72 was built.

FAVOURITE ALBUM: *Closer* by Joy Division is my all-time greatest album. My inability to listen to this album without it scaring me is proof of its sheer brilliance. The album is almost operatic in its drama, a bastion of the human condition made beautiful.

39

JOE DOLAN

Born in Mullingar, County Westmeath, Joe Dolan has become an Irish music phenomenon. Since forming his first band in 1964 his successful musical career has flourished through five decades and his energetic live performances have spawned the now immortal line "There's No Show Like a Joe Show!" From his first release, 'The Answer To Everything' in 1964, Joe has enjoyed enormous chart success, and such well known anthems as 'Make Me An Island', 'You're Such A Good-looking Woman' and 'More and More' have sealed Joe Dolan's name in Irish music history. Nor has his success been restricted to the Irish circuit. His countless overseas achievements include legendary residencies in Las Vegas, scoring four UK charts hits (including 'Make Me An Island' and 'You're Such A Good-looking Woman'), performing on BBC television's *Top of the Pops* and, in 1978, earning the accolade of being the first western artist to play live in Russia. He still performs over 200 concerts a year and continues to attract the adulation of both young and old.

" My earliest memory of music can be traced back to when I was very young, possibly four or five when I sat listening to people playing Irish music in our house in Mullingar. At that time, our house was a regular meeting place for Irish musicians, especially at the weekends. My mother would play the fiddle and I would sit around listening to all the tunes she and the others would play. So through those informal get-togethers I was introduced to the wonderful world of music for the first time.

The radio was probably the next most influential source of music for me. I remember listening to Elvis Presley as a teenager, and to other stars such as Jerry Lee Lewis, Brenda Lee and Frankie Laine. Thinking back I'd say it was Elvis who was the one I most wanted to emulate. I'm sure I wasn't the only one he inspired in this way.

The first gig I went to was to see the Clipper Carlton Showband from Strabane in County Tyrone. They were one of the first-ever show bands. It was just an amazing gig and it had quite an effect on me, not least in relation to the career path I was to follow. I never wanted to be a Garda or a teacher or anything like that. I served my time as a compositor with the *Westmeath Examiner* newspaper, but became more and more attracted to music as time went by, and more and more began to feel that music would be the right career for me.

The first gig I played was in the Parochial Hall in Castletown Geoghegan in County Westmeath. It was our first night with The Drifters Showband, which had been formed by my brother Ben and myself. I suppose you could say I 'drifted' into music!

I have had so many great moments throughout my career, but it's the simple concert that gets me every time. Every time I go out on that stage is 'the best moment' for me as a singer. At no time have I wanted to pack it in. I have never ever felt so frustrated as to think of saying goodbye to the music business. I just love it too much."

FAVOURITE ARTIST:
I have many favourites, like The Rolling Stones and Elvis but maybe if I were pushed I'd go for Ella Fitzgerald. Her singing has always sent a shiver down my spine. Other top favourites include U2, Coldplay and Mick Jagger.

40

JOHN SPILLANE

John Spillane is a native of Cork, and that county, which he lovingly describes as 'the centre of the universe', has been a huge influence on this popular singer-songwriter. John is quite a unique vocalist, with an almost *sean-nós* element to a voice that has been described as 'full of honesty, commitment and sensitivity'. After a spell with the highly regarded folk outfit, Nomos, his debut solo album, *The Wells of the World*, was released in 1997 to general acclaim. It was described in *Hot Press* as 'a striking and individual musical statement.' His compositions have been summarised as highly original in concept, full of imagery and wonder. He won the prestigious Realta 2001 Irish song contest and his influences over the years include John Lennon, Bob Dylan, Joni Mitchell and Leonard Cohen.

" It seems to me that certain moments in life are more vivid than others. I have a very vivid memory of when I was four years old, crawling on the footpath singing "my bonny lies over the ocean", and singing it over and over again.

And I said to myself, "This was feckin' great!" I discovered that when you get to the end you could start all over again. I realised then (just like I *know* now) that I loved singing. Any time I was on my own I would sing and sing and sing.

I first learned to play an instrument at school. It was the tin whistle, although they called it the flageolet. The teacher wasn't very good at it. We learned the first part of a tune and then the thing just fell to pieces. So it was a bad introduction really. I never thought I was any good at music and I got no real music training at school. But one day, maybe when I was eight or nine, a guy came into the class and he taught us the DO-RE-MI. He wrote it on the board, DO-RE-MI-FA-SO-LA-TI-DO, and then he told us that you can sing it up and you can sing it down, or you can sing DO-MI-SO-DO or you can try and go straight from DO to LA, whatever you want. That half-hour education has done me all my life. That's all I needed to know about music. I'm exaggerating a little, but I always think like this. I can read music, I play bass now, I'm good at harmonies, I can arrange music, but I still think in basic DO RE MI. I loved singing since then and often when I was on my own I would sing for pleasure just like when I was a child.

Another thing that appealed to me was storytelling. You would get young fellas from my gang into the garage up the road and entertain them with stories. It's the same as writing songs, which tell a story in a different way.

Although I loved singing I didn't think I was any good at music. I had a brother Maurice (Mossy) who was older and better then me and I never thought that I could pick up tunes by ear like he could. It would take me a good while to find the notes whereas he could find the tune straight away. But when I was about fifteen I used to mess around with a guitar he had, and it started from there. He didn't keep up the guitar for very long. He just learned a few chords then left it. There were only four strings on it, the third and fourth string were missing. I also found a song book of Simon and Garfunkel's greatest hits lying around with the words of all the songs, as well as chord diagrams and I learned to play and sing each song in it.

Another memory that stayed with me is of going down to the Gaeltacht in Banangerry in the summer of 1977. I was fifteen and there was a bunch of lads down there from Dublin. They thought they were really cool and that we were culchies from Cork. They were into Bob Dylan and the Rolling Stones and they could play the guitar and they were way ahead of us. I learned my first song on the guitar from them - the song from Pink Floyd that starts with the words "The lunatic is on the grass". Yes, the Jackeens were a great education to us - and Heffo's army hadn't even risen yet!

From then on I played the guitar for hours on end. I fell madly in love with it. I'd come home from school at lunchtime and play through the afternoon, and I went through various stages of learning from different albums. I spent about six months learning 'Blackbird' by the Beatles which has very fancy guitar playing. I'd put the needle on the record and learn one note at a time. I'm obviously good for the long haul and for persevering!

Music and writing are a kind of mystery. If you knew how to keep writing successful songs you would make a fortune. The first song that I ever wrote was when I was eight or nine years old and it was all about "Plodding". I would walk around saying, "plodding, plodding, plodding"! It was a good song as there was only one word in it! It had a certain rhythm to it!

My inspiration for songs is always to think through poetry, think of the song as a poem. If I get a good idea I can make a song out of it. But the best think you can do with an idea for a song is to leave it there, let it ferment in the back of your mind and then when you come to it later you can be better at it, even if it might be years later.

I think traditional Irish music, roots music, is really power-ful. It's like rock and roll, music that came from black African music, mixed with white music. There's a deep well from where that type of music comes. It's a deep source, so no wonder it conquered the world. I think it's the same with Trad music. Some people think it belongs to the past, that it hasn't even happened yet and at some stage it's just going to erupt and take the world by storm. It'll happen when the time is right. It belongs to the future. It just needs that Bob Marley-type figure to take it to the whole wide world."

41

JULIET TURNER

Juliet Turner was born in Tummery, Co Tyrone. She was, she admits, "a bit of a performer" as a child. But she began to take singing seriously only in 1993 while she was studying at Trinity College in Dublin. In 1996 she recorded her first batch of songs, which would result in her debut album, *Let's Hear It For Pizza*. Having gained worldwide acclaim from her emotional performance at the Omagh bombing remembrance concert, Juliet released her second album, *Burn The Black Suit*, which went on to sell 40,000 copies in Ireland. In an action-packed career Juliet has to date shared stages with some of the most respected acts in the music world, including U2, Bob Dylan, Tracy Chapman, Sting, Art Garfunkel, Steve Earle, Luka Bloom, Mary Coughlan, David Essex and Altan, as well as countless headlining spots with her own band.

" The first person to really influence me as a songwriter was Jimmy MacCarthy. I used to listen to a lot of his music when I was a teenager. When you are at that age you enjoy that kind of melancholy and his music really hit me when I was about sixteen or seventeen. I just thought that he created an incredible marriage of lyric and melody. It was not so much folk music as sheer poetry. At that time I had no idea that I was going to end up doing what I do now. I didn't have any leanings towards a music career, but Jimmy was definitely the artist I listened to most. When I was younger I knew I wanted to write in some shape or form. I was always getting caught in corners and up trees writing poems and stories. But I never imagined that it would be something that I would do seriously as a career. I always figured I would end up as a teacher, or something along those lines, and when I entered the university in Dublin I started off as a speech and language therapist.

The strange thing is that I never really listened to a lot of music when I was a teenager. In fact I think I probably skipped that whole thing. But in the family house there was a mix of Irish ballads and country music. I heard Hank Williams, Dolly Parton and Johnny Cash because that was what my parents listened to. I was never a cool teenager like my friends who were into Depeche Mode and A-Ha. For some reason I never clicked into that at all.

My parents bought me my first guitar when I was fifteen and I became intrigued by the idea of performing and the power that music gave you in that respect. I didn't get stuck into it until a friend of mine in my second year in college heard me singing and asked me to try out at a local venue called the Living Room and it just took off from there.

When I first started gigging I remember being eaten up by nerves, but it was never so bad that it would hold me back. I would often forget the lyrics but I'd just keep going or start again. My 'Living Room University' friend advised me that I should start writing my own songs because he said I'd never be able to make a living from it unless I wrote my own music. He was the first person who ever seriously believed that I could go for it. So I started slipping my own songs in amidst the cover songs at these gigs and it was then that I found that connection, like when I had listened to Jimmy MacCarthy's music and saw how you can marry your lyrics to lovely melodies, and, lo and behold, you have a beautiful song! For me there's a weird alchemy to it, the way in which everything came together for me. I had finally found a way of expressing myself that sat right with me.

I went to a weekend songwriting workshop a few years ago and Jimmy MacCarthy was there. At the time I didn't even know what he looked like, and to meet him was really amazing. One of the highlights of my life was to sit next to him in a pub and he just lifted up the guitar and began singing these beautiful songs that I grew up listening to, like 'The Bright Blue Rose' and 'Katie'. I cried and sang along having never expected to find myself actually singing these songs with the person who wrote them, songs that had such a profound effect on me when I was growing up.

The first gig I ever went to, and this might be a bit uncool, was Chris De Burgh in the King's Hall in Belfast. It was great. He had a great band and it was the first time I'd ever seen anyone on a stage like that. But one concert that influenced me profoundly was Christie Hennessy in the Opera House in Belfast. That gig blew me away because it was almost like being in someone's house with everyone so relaxed. I never knew that a concert could be like that, with all that mystery and performance, while still being very inclusive of the audience. That influenced me a lot in the way I approached my early gigs.

There's definitely a sense that music chose me, I didn't choose it. Everything fell into place almost immediately. I never had to shop around for a record deal or a manager. Everything just went 'plop' into my lap, although I would never say it was fate - that would be too grandiose a statement. My safety net has always been my degree and I'm perfectly willing to accept the fact that sooner or later people are going to lose interest and that I'm going to have to find another way of making money. But if it stops, if there's no longer an audience, I wonder if I will keep writing songs, because the whole buzz of writing songs is that other people get to hear them. Anyway, I never take it for granted that this is what I'll be doing for the rest of my life.

I'm the kind of person who goes with the flow and with what's happening now. I get really fired up about my writing, but I suppose that's the Northern Protestant in me, very sensible and very practical, enjoying it while I can, and working as hard as I can. But nothing in this life can be taken for granted."

42

KIERAN GOSS

Kieran Goss was born in 1962 in Newry, County Down, the tenth in a family of fifteen. He studied law at Queen's University, Belfast, but after qualifying as a lawyer in 1985 he turned his back on a legal career to concentrate on song-writing and became one of the biggest selling home-based recording artists in the country. Kieran has to date released five albums - four solo albums, and one duo album with Frances Black, plus a very successful *Best Of*. His album, *Worse Than Pride*, went straight into the number 7 slot in the charts in the first week of its release and sold 30,000 copies in nine months, thereby achieving double platinum status. The album also yielded two Top 20 singles and stayed in the Top 50 for nine months.

" There was no single defining moment that made music my career, but I recall a certain atmosphere that I was attracted to and it came from music. When I was eight my older brothers and sisters were into the Beatles and the Rolling Stones. Country music was big then, as was country and Irish.

My father played the accordion and was passionate about céili bands. My mother loved classic American ballads, Frank Sinatra, Cole Porter, Tony Bennett. I heard great songs like 'Night and Day' when I was too young to know whether they were good or bad.

When I was nine I got an acoustic guitar for Christmas. My first performance was for my parents' Silver Wedding anniversary when I was 11. The first song I played for them was 'Crazy Horses' by the Osmonds. There I was in my crappy little suit thinking I was great because I could slide bar chords! But it brought me attention and that felt good. I'd see folksy guitar-playing singer-songwriters on television - James Taylor, Tom Paxton, Jim Croce, Paul Simon - and my older brother Liam taught me some of their songs. But with my first band, Nightshift, I did Thin Lizzy and Free covers. You grew your hair long, pretended you had some attitude and played as loud as you could. It was great! It made you learn, because you had to play Thin Lizzy solos properly.

I guested with showbands in Newry if they needed a guitar player, mainly doing country and western. You tried to look bored and cool, but you took the money! Then at university I started to develop my own songwriting. The Beatles inspired me to write good lyrics, and the basic structure of my songs is no different from their songs, or those written by, say, Aimee Mann, Ron Sexsmith or Crowded House.

There was no support structure for a budding singer-songwriter then in rural County Down. Luckily, the Sands family lived nearby and they were getting much recognition in the Irish folk world. Imagine, a band from just down the road playing Carnegie Hall! I realised you could be from Mayo Bridge and take your music to the world.

Everything you do helps your music. When I was a student I played songs like 'American Pie' and 'Hey, Jude' in pubs.

Playing music made me happy and became even more important when I started writing. I could sit for hours working out songs by James Taylor, or Freddie White's 'Tenderness On The Block'. It wasn't a technical thing, as I hate guitar solos. They're boring unless there's something sublime in there. But I get off on chords, irrespective of whether it's the Beatles or some uncool pop band.

I might not have been able to articulate the attraction of songwriting, but I loved it. It wasn't work; it wasn't studying. Good songwriting touches people. When I write I go for songs that will have meaning in someone's life, not songs that try to impress. As you mature you realise that the incidents in your life also happen in other people's lives. When a song is personal I think it's also universal. I love that quality. I write very simply because that's what really gets me most. It's about being true to your talent and true to your vision.

Johnny Cash and Willie Nelson were also influences. Paul McCartney has a sense of melody that touches me, melodies no one else can write. History will claim he wrote his best songs when he was under twenty-five. For some writers it happens early, for others much later. Johnny Cash reached seventy and was doing some of the best music of his life. That's encouraging for me in my early forties, since every career musician has to deal with the dilemma of whether to become more formulaic and more predictable, or to plough their own furrow.

What I do has nothing to do with *Popstars* or Westlife. That kind of packaged pop is always around, like the Osmonds or Bay City Rollers. But the people I admire are often outside of what Joe Public thinks is the music world. What I do belongs to a world with artists like Rodney Crowell, Paul Brady, Willie Nelson, Elvis Costello, and I put marketing second. You can choose to be either an artist or a star. Only a few can do both, like Madonna. If you try to be both you might achieve neither.

So maybe you don't keep going for the number one just for the sake of it and you don't play the fame game because it's fickle.

The biggest turning point for me was giving up my solicitor's job when I was twenty-five. I had qualified, but I didn't want to grow old in an office in Newry. I felt too young in myself. So I gave up law and travelled around Germany, France and the USA. I put a line between my past and what was going to be my future. It gave me space from the day-to-day head-wreck of a job I didn't want to do and wasn't going to make me happy.

It's a gut feeling, knowing when you've done something right even if others think you're crazy, and making the most of your talent. You become happier, the people around you are happier, you're easier to be with and you attract people you want to attract - open-minded, artistic, creative people.

Music isn't my whole life, but it's a very important part of it. My life's about growth, staying close to people I love and want to be with. Music fits into the picture of what I want from life. When I'm old I hope I can look back on a body of work and feel proud I wrote those songs and made great albums that will last and that doing it didn't separate me from those I love."

43

KILA

Ronan Ó Snodaigh, singer, instrumentalist

Multi-instrumentalist Ronan Ó Snodaigh plays bodhran, djembe, congas, bongos, guitar and sings with Kila of which he was a founder member in October 1987. An accomplished prize-winning poet (in both Irish and English), adding rhythm to his oration helped form his percussive chant-like singing style. He has created a unique bodhran style which often evokes African talking drums or Indian tables. He played, toured and recorded with Dead Can Dance among several other bands, before Kila was born. Ronan recently recorded twelve of his English language songs for future release. He is generally credited with having invented Kila's name but when asked what it means or where it comes from he tends to give a different answer each time!

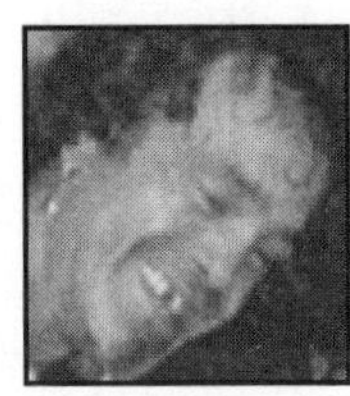

" My most vivid memory of music from my childhood was the rhythm of my cradle rocking when I was a baby. Radio acted as a big influence on me in a variety of ways; I really enjoyed the music played on pirate radio stations in the eighties. When they were banned and disappeared from the airways I stopped listening to the radio altogether and started buying records instead and really discovered music for myself.

My parents don't actually come from a musical background but they used to collect music from different parts of the world whenever they visited and through that I was exposed to a lot of different types of music.

I can't remember the first gig I went to, but my older brother taught me and my friend how to bunk in for free into the RDS.

Kila's first gig was for the Pioneer Society in Bray, Co. Wicklow. It was hilarious! The first gig I really enjoyed, or felt was very special was supporting bodhran player Damien Quinn. He was a big idol of mine.

When I was growing up it was my intention to be a footballer (with Manchester United) and I dedicated all my time and energy towards that specific end. At fifteen, however, I had an operation on my knee and the course of my football career was changed somewhat.

One of the best moments to date for me as a member of Kila was when we were playing in France during the late eighties. After our gig had ended we met a band called Ar Re Yaouank (a Breton band) in a hotel lobby. Both bands started to play together spontaneously with hardly any talking beforehand. We played until about five o'clock in the morning in the hotel lobby and did the same again the following night. I played faster on those nights than I've played before or since. A friend of one of our girlfriends at the time, who had never really seen live musicians playing before, became so moved that she started crying.

Playing on the streets has given me some of my best and most memorable moments. At times there could be up to thirty of us busking together in Dublin.

I've been asked if there's ever been a time when the heavy workload has made me feel frustrated and when I might have had enough of the music business. It happens all the time, just last week in fact."

FAVOURITE SONG: 'I've Got You Back' by Mic Christopher who died tragically a year ago in Holland.

FAVOURITE BAND: Toto El Monpasina from Colombia.

FAVOURITE ALBUM: *The Pearl* by Brian Eno and Harold Budd

44

LESLEY DOWDALL

As lead vocalist with the band In Tua Nua, Lesley Dowdall scaled the heights of rock success, garnering hit singles and albums, countless awards and much acclaim all across Europe. After the band's demise, Dowdall set up her own record label on which she released two albums of mostly self-penned songs including the hit single 'Wonderful Thing'. More recently, that song has featured in several television campaigns for the National Lottery, and Dowdall herself has been guesting with Paul Brady and Van Morrison.

" There was always a piano in our house as a piece of furniture, even though nobody could play it. So I tended to doodle around on it. My earliest childhood memories include being lambasted by my aunt because I used to make up my own chords when I was playing around with the piano. That was when I was about eleven, and I thought I was brilliant! I used to play songs like 'Rhinestone Cowboy'. My mother was an actress, a child star in the Gate Theatre in

Dublin, but she didn't really sing. Neither did either of my brothers. My father was a lovely singer, a crooner, and played double bass with a jazz band in London. He wouldn't need his arm twisted at events like weddings before he'd get up and give us a song. My father played jazz records at home and we listened to the radio a lot, but I don't recall any specific influences from either. The record collection included all sorts of stuff, from Dave Brubeck jazz albums to the *Sound Of Music* soundtrack.

I think the musicals attracted me most at that time. I loved watching musicals on television, with people like Ginger Rogers and Fred Astaire. From there I got into tap dancing and singing at the same time when I was maybe nine! I also remember coming into the house and announcing that I was now a mouth-organ player! I'd bought a cheap mouth organ and I proceeded to give an impromptu performance on it. I wasn't shy, that's for sure!

After we moved from Dublin to Rathvilly in County Carlow I spotted a poster advertising a local talent competition for under-fifteens. When I told the family I was planning to enter there were great gusts of laughter. Undeterred, off I went on my Raleigh bike. I think the adjudicator was a champion Irish dancer. I sang 'Leaving On a Jet Plane' by John Denver and won first prize of an autograph book, and my victory was announced at Mass!

Regular gigs didn't really exist where we lived, but we went to the occasional musical. At school I sang in Gilbert and Sullivan's *Trial By Jury* and stuff like that. I went to piano lessons with the nuns, but I never learned to sight-read. I played by ear then, and still do. I started to play the guitar as well, and sang songs like Bob Dylan's 'Blowin' In The Wind' and songs by John Denver. I picked them up from the radio or from simple chord books. I didn't have guitar lessons. I should have!

When I was about 16, I went to the USA where I worked at all kinds of jobs, from waitressing to registering cot deaths. While there I was taken by some Filipino friends to a classical concert and I think that was the first time I felt I wanted to be a serious performer on stage and maybe make a career of it.

When I finished at school I attended Art College where I joined the folk club. The first album I'd bought had been Joni Mitchell's *Blue*. I loved her song 'Carey'. We'd go to places like the Coffee Kitchen in Dublin to perform, usually in return for free mugs of coffee. I did bluesy-folk gigs with two guys, one who played fantastic boogie-woogie piano but never played a song the same way twice, and a guitar player and college colleague Conor Kelly who was later in a band called Max.

A major musical influence was my teenage obsession with Horslips. I went to all their concerts and had a complete crush on their fiddle player Charles O'Connor. I thought he was the coolest man I'd ever seen! At some point I stayed in a flat with some girls from Monaghan and one of their brothers was in a band called The Electric Maggots, so I played with them for a while. One of the guys was Henry Gillanders who runs Piano Plus, the instrument shop, and we once did a demo in Big Tom's studio.

I then placed an advertisement in *Hot Press* looking for people to form a band. One of the replies was from a bunch of guys who arranged to meet me at 7 am outside a public toilet in Ranelagh. In my innocence they took me in a Ford Cortina to a dodgy warehouse where they played me some U2 songs like 'I Will Follow'. That wasn't for me.

My next spell was with The Assembly who later became The Gorehounds. Brian O'Kelly, who ran the Comet Record shops, was our keyboard player, although he actually played a stylophone. Ray Harmon, not the Something Happens guy, played bass, plus a guy called Kenny on guitar and we had a drum machine. We did demos and Fanning Sessions for 2FM, gigged at venues like the Ivy Rooms and supported Rocky de Valera and The Rhythm Kings at the Baggot Inn. I toured with Rocky as guest vocalist and they used to introduce me as Síle de Valera! We played at my twenty-first birthday party when we were living in Bunclody, which was odd in that our stuff was quite downbeat, hardly 'happy birthday' material. While my father was bringing out the birthday cake we were singing some depressing dirge about "walking down the street and wanting to get sick". My brother thought we were crap, but we thought we were avant-garde.

After college I worked in an advertising agency until my boss advised me to forget about a career in that industry as she could see I was much more interested in music. Ivan O'Shea was working in Eamon Andrews Studio as a recording engineer and he heard a demo I'd recorded there with The Assembly. He was part of the nucleus of In Tua Nua in Howth and he recommended me and I joined what was an eight-piece band with sax and uillean pipes. After our first gig in 1982 at the TV Club in Harcourt Street we got signed to Island Records almost immediately and in due course we recorded three albums.

After the band broke up amid much litigation, I gave up music for a while and came back to work on my solo career."

MAIN INFLUENCES: Joni Mitchell, James Taylor

FAVOURITE SONG: Maybe 'Carey' by Joni Mitchell

FAVOURITE ALBUMS: *Blue* by Joni Mitchell and *Rumours* by Fleetwood Mac

FAVOURITE SONGWRITER: I like American songwriters like Dylan, Springsteen, Lyle Lovett and Shawn Colvin because they tell wonderful stories set into great musical landscapes.

45

LUAN
PARLE

Luan Parle was born in County Wicklow in 1981, her distinctive surname derived from a French ancestor who was shipwrecked off the Wexford coast. Luan began to develop her own vocal style early on in life, and only a few months before her seventh birthday she won the first of a string of talent contests. Signed to Sony Music on a worldwide deal in 2001, she is blessed with one of the strongest and most distinctive contemporary vocal styles to emerge onto the Irish music scene in recent years. So it came as no surprise to music industry insiders when in 2002 she was snapped up by Elton John's manager, Derek Mackillop, who puts her in the same league as hot American star LeAnn Rimes.

❜❜ My earliest memories of music revolve around bedtime. Normally, kids are read stories to help put them to sleep, but when I was a tot we were sung to sleep. We wouldn't go to sleep unless our dad came and sit at the end of the bed and sang nursery rhymes and the like. And we would sing along too. I can remember songs like "Jimmy crack corn and I don't care", all sorts of songs like that. My dad was a great singer, one of the best, and in my eyes he *is* the best. He trained me since I was a tot. He was my inspiration and my everything really.

Later, I had all my idols available to me on the telly too. I grew up watching Kylie Minogue, and as far as I was concerned she was the bee's knees! My dad would often sit down to sing songs and I would sit down with him. When I was about six I asked him to teach me how to play the guitar. It was at that age that I started to enter talent competitions. I have a recording of the first one on video and on it you can see me singing and my friend playing guitar for me. I sang a song called 'Two Little Orphans'. I tried really hard for the sympathy vote, but I still didn't win!

My dad has always tried to help me with my singing and my music career, and we have had all the usual arguments and disagreements about different aspects of music and performing. When you admire certain singers like I did back then, singers like Kylie Minogue and others of similar talent, you really do look up to them. You want to be them. You have their posters on your wall and you listen out for them on the radio. I was even in the Kylie Minogue fan club. I had the books, the whole lot.

I never remember a moment when I took some time to think things over and decided, "Yes this is what I want to do". One thing simply led naturally to another, from singing nursery rhymes to singing in the church to singing for an audience. It was a natural progress, just something I loved doing. If you put me up in front of a crowd anywhere at any time I would be in my element. Even when I'm tired there has never ever been a time when I've thought to myself that I don't want to do this any more. I really am delighted to be doing what I'm doing.

My parents are my main influences. They've been behind me all the way. Of course there have been times when they have made the right decision even though I would have disagreed with them at the time. For instance, when I was thirteen I was offered a record deal with a company in Nashville. I had just started secondary school and I was telling all my friends that I was moving over to Nashville and that I was going to be a star. But after careful consideration my parents thought that I should finish my leaving certificate studies first and that we should decline the offer. I disagreed. I thought this might be my one big chance and that by turning it down they were ruining my life. But we made a deal - if I went back and finished school and then still wanted to be a professional singer they promised they would support me one hundred per cent.

I know now that this was a very sensible decision, but the next day I had to go to school and tell my mates that my plans for stardom were going to have to wait a little while longer.

Looking to the future, I hope to be very successful and I want to keep writing my own songs. But at the end of the day it's nice to have a few quid in the back pocket as well!"

46

LUKA BLOOM

Kevin Barry Moore was born on 23rd May 1955 to Nancy Power and Andy Moore of Newbridge in County Kildare. He is the youngest member of the family and has three sisters and two brothers, one of whom is none other than the legendary Christy Moore himself. Having recorded albums for two major record labels, Warners and Sony, his albums and singles have appeared in charts as far away as Singapore. More recently he has set up his own record label on which he released the acclaimed album, *Between The Mountain And The Moon*.

" One memory that is very personal to me is of singing an Irish song called '*Dílín O Damhasa*' in the *Feis* Matthew back when I was five years of age. I came home in second place, and I remember being absolutely horrified, disgusted and distraught at the fact that I didn't win the shagging thing! But a fonder memory I have is of singing a song called 'My Singing Bird' which would have been one of the first songs that I ever learned. It's a beautiful song and I remember singing it in the Palace Cinema in Newbridge in Co Kildare, again around the age of seven or eight. I can't remember whether it was a competition or not, but I walked out with a Christmas pudding anyway. I didn't go home empty handed! I didn't nick it, honest, I won it! It was the first time that I made the connection between singing and being rewarded just because of the music. I didn't show any great potential in the football department or the sporting department either, but I had the *grá* for the singing from the very beginning.

Music was always there in the family and my mother was an amazing woman. She gave me and the whole family a great love of music. She was quite a rare kind of person in that when people came into the house, and she was in the right mood, music would just begin to happen. The house would be filled with singing as if it was the most natural thing to do. God love you, but even if you didn't have a note in your head she just wouldn't let you out until you sang a song. So she instilled in all of us a great love of music. I feel like it was in my blood and I can still remember to this day the very first time I held a guitar. I'll never forget that moment of magic, the first time I sat down and held a guitar, and I've been playing guitar ever since.

These are memories of very precious moments in my life, memories that constantly remind me of why I got into this business in the first place. People ask me all the time "What in the name of God possessed you to be drawn in to the music world?" It's not unusual to be asked these questions ten or fifteen times a year, and I actually don't mind it because I love being reminded of the innocent hunger that I had for this job. It makes me realise how fortunate I was to be given this gift at such a young age.

My brother Christy was living in England when I was about thirteen or fourteen. He would have started playing at folk clubs around that time. Part of the arrangement every summer was for poor oul' Christy to take me off our mother's hands and babysit me for the two weeks. This meant that on one or two occasions I went off to England and travelled around English folk clubs. So I soon had a repertoire of seven or eight songs on the guitar and by the time I was seventeen I became the first opening act that Planxty ever had.

My mother was keen to see we got a good education, but my heart wasn't it. I got my Leaving Cert in Newbridge College but immediately dropped out. I made a couple of attempts to go to university, but only to please my mother, and I got kicked out of Trinity College after one year. Then I got kind of kicked out of the University of Limerick too and it became obvious to everybody by about 1976 that I was never going to get to be a second-year student, let alone get a degree. People gradually surrendered to the fact that what I really wanted was to get serious about playing music.

I had very specific influences, and the most important ones in my early years pointed me in the direction of writing songs. So I was writing my own songs by the time I was thirteen. My sister Eilis gave me my first guitar; my brother Christy bought me my first serious guitar. But from about fourteen onwards I came under the spell of the singer-songwriters. Not so much Bob Dylan, but people like Neil Young, James Taylor and Joni Mitchell, possibly because of their distinctive guitar styles. People who wrote simple songs but who had a very distinctive way of playing the guitar appealed to me.

I can't actually pinpoint a specific moment when I felt music would definitely be my calling I suppose it started for me in Joe O'Rourke's in the backstreets of Newbridge when I was sixteen. And I wasn't singing ballads or Rolling Stone songs, I was singing my own songs and it was obvious to me that that was the way to go. I had an audience of ten or fifteen people every Friday night. They were listening to my songs and we had a great time. I didn't really need that definitive moment; it was written, as they would say, in the Koran.

People sometimes ask me where do I go on from here, what does the future hold for me. There's a great old saying that if you want to give God a good laugh just tell him your plans. If anyone had told me fifteen years ago that I would change my name to Luka Bloom, that I would live in America, or that I would have deals with major record companies, I would have said, "Yeah and pigs can fly!". But that's what happened, so who knows what the future will bring? In the meantime, I'm just getting on with my life. Making music is what I do."

47

LUKE THOMAS

Born in Dublin, twenty-year-old Luke Thomas is rated as one of Ireland's top R'n'B artists. Now an acclaimed songwriter, singer and rapper, Luke tasted success at an early age. His first-ever performance was in Trinidad where he entered, and won, a talent contest while visiting the island on holiday at the age of six. At the age of fifteen he was selected to support superstar rapper Coolio's concert in Dublin. Luke's vocal talents have been compared by many to established hit-makers like Craig David and Usher. He has already had two top-ten Irish hit singles, and 2002 saw him scoop a Meteor Irish Music Award for *Best Dance Act*. The future looks bright indeed for this talented young performer.

’’I remember waking up on Sunday mornings hearing my mother downstairs in the kitchen listening to her favourite music by artists like Stevie Wonder, Bob Marley and Lionel Richie. That has to be my earliest memory of music. My dad would have been into Neil Diamond, Cliff Richard and

The Beatles, so it was a musically diverse household I was born into.

When I went to Trinidad for the first time, I think when I was six or seven, I was exposed for the first time to local steel bands. I became really interested in that sort of music, so I didn't particularly want to be a singer straight away. But I soon wanted to be some kind of a performer or work somewhere in the entertainment business. But it was only in secondary school that I began to take this ambition seriously. I became a member of a rap group to start off with in third year. I still didn't take singing seriously until somebody told me at a pop showcase gig that I should try singing. People had often said to me, "Your rapping is great, but you're not in America! Would you not try singing?" I was fourteen at the time and I was doing showcases where people like Brian McFadden of Westlife and Samantha Mumba would also be performing.

I've always believed in myself and I've had five or six different managers down through the years. You get so many knock-backs, people promising you the world but delivering nothing. When I was fifteen, if I saw people on the telly who I'd once been on the same stage with, like Brian McFadden, I would say to myself "Hopefully, one day that will be me". I was so determined to keep at it.

Apart from my family, Michael Jackson has always been a massive influence on me. His whole performance, his whole package, just everything about him is so inspirational. I was quite young during the 1980s when he was at his peak, but when I got a bit older I got round to listening to his recordings much more closely. In terms of entertainment value I reckon there's no one to touch him.

For a while when I was younger I wanted to be a teacher. I wanted to be creative, so I didn't go to any performing arts school or to the famous Billy Barry School. I just wanted to do something different, something that came out of me and not imposed on me from outside. Immediately before I met my current managers, Vibe Music, I didn't know what to do with myself. I had other managers who had promised me the world, but they had no money to invest in my career, just waffled away to me that they knew this person or knew that person, as if that's all it would take.

But deep down inside I've always had this belief in myself that eventually I'll get there. Getting the Meteor Award and having the two top-ten hits convinced me I was going in the right direction. In periods of disappointment I've told myself I shouldn't be feeling down, that I'm getting there slowly but surely. So it's encouraging the way things are going now. It's a tough business and nothing like the fairyland picture you get from those television 'reality' shows.

If you work hard, you'll end up with some brilliant memories. The first time I heard my song on the radio, it really meant something to me. It was a very special moment and it sent shivers up my spine, a song that I wrote being broadcast on the radio. So I work harder, and I aim higher. If I fall short, I'll always know I've tried my best."

FAVOURITE ALBUM: *Thriller* by Michael Jackson

FAVOURITE SONGS: 'Billie Jean' by Michael Jackson

48

MARIA DOYLE KENNEDY

Maria Doyle Kennedy first began singing with the band Hothouse Flowers and she recorded their first single 'Love Don't Work This Way' with them. She then recorded two albums with the Black Velvet Band, *When Justice Came* and *King Of Myself*. While working on their second album she successfully auditioned for a role as a member of the now famous band in the film *The Commitments*. The movie was directed by Alan Parker and became a worldwide hit towards the end of the eighties. Over the years, Maria has enjoyed further acting success with roles in several films, and 2002 saw her release her debut solo album, *Charm*.

"When I was five I saw *The Wizard Of Oz* film in a big school hall, with a big old projector. I guess that's what struck me first, both musically and visually, as a child. I suppose the memory is magnified a hundred times in my mind because I was so small, and it absolutely blew my mind, the colour, the music and the costumes. I can still see the whole hall and all these tiny kids just sitting there watching the huge screen. Actually, the reel broke down in the middle. I was holding my breath for days afterwards, I was so moved by it. When I was small I always sang to myself. I picked up whatever was on the radio, or whatever my dad played on his car radio. My mother said that she could always tell what kind of mood I was in. When the mood was good there was a lot of noise around the place, but silence was never a good sign!

My parents weren't a particularly big influence for me when I was growing up. My father always had music on in his car, but it was what I'd call 'Dad music', artists like Roger Whittaker and Frank Sinatra. I think loads of that stuff is great. He would listen to The Carpenters too, and their melodies are amazing. When I was about fourteen we went away for a weekend and on the way back he bought a Billie Holiday album for me. I don't know why he bought it, because it was totally out of character. But this album completely revolutionised my music listening; I had never heard anything like it before, and Billie became a huge inspiration for me.

I used to go to my friends' houses when I was ten or eleven. We would set up the tape recorder and tape the pop charts from the radio every Sunday around six o'clock. We would listen to that tape all through the following week. I remember when we were dying to hear the Sex Pistols' single, 'God Save the Queen', but unfortunately it was banned from the radio. When I was fourteen we got a stereo player for the family at Christmas. It was like a seventies three-in-one, a brown posh one like a mini-table. I got Joni Mitchell's album *Court and Spark* and Bob Dylan's *Street Legal* 'off Santa'. But the next day my *Street Legal* was stolen at a party. But I listened to the Joni Mitchell album forever, and I know every word of every song. I still think that album is amazing, great melodies and words that make you think, with ideas that weren't handed to you on a plate. You had to use your ears and use your mind.

The next big thing was Patti Smith. She is my absolute idol. She is such a beacon in the 'walk your own road' department. It wasn't that she always knew exactly what to do, but she certainly always knew what she didn't like, and was really strong about it. And she seemed to never compromise. I had first heard Patti when I was about fourteen and somebody's older brother played what would become a big hit for her, 'Because the Night', which she wrote with Bruce Springsteen. I thought it was amazing. But I didn't hear anything about her for years and then Maria McKee, who herself had a big hit single with 'Show Me Heaven', played her album to me one day when we were stuck in a traffic jam. But I disliked it so much I wanted to turn it off and Maria laughed her head off and said, 'You'll get it eventually''. About six months later I picked up that album, put it on and never looked back.

I'm at my happiest playing to live audiences, that's when the realisation hits home that I'm doing what I love. I love writing songs too; I love finding a little word or a melody in my head and then making something of it. I love recording because you get the chance to work with lots of talented people, to collaborate with them to turn a fragment you've written into a complete song on record. I love all of that, but music means most to me when I'm actually singing live to people who are there in the room. You just have those moments at a gig, whether it's your gig or somebody's else's gig, where you just feel plugged in to the whole thing and you feel you are sharing something special with a load of other people.

It was like that for the very first gig I went to, The Blades in the Mississippi Rooms in Bray. I was underage, but I snuck in and it was absolutely amazing. There's nothing like a proper live gig. And that's the magic for me really, and when I did it myself for the first time there was no going back.

I always wanted to sing and felt I had to sing. I never thought of it as a profession, because I didn't really know anything about that side of it. I didn't know anybody else who made music or was in a band. I bought records and I was always listening to music. It was a huge part of my life and still is. I find it mind-boggling when I meet some people and music isn't really part of their lives. They never buy CD's, they don't have it on in their cars, and they don't go to gigs. I think ''How do you get through the day!!!'' ''

FAVOURITE ALBUM: If I'm pushed, one of my favourite albums is Jeff Buckley's album, *Grace*. It's outrageously beautiful. It would definitely be the one I'd grab from a burning house.

49

METISSE
Skully

Skully from County Cork formed the highly successful band Metisse with his partner Aida in 1997. Their artistic partnership mixes Skully's flamboyant musical talents and Aida's sensational singing abilities. That partnership has seen their songs used at The Olympic Games, in various advertisements and on several soundtracks, including Madonna's *Next Best Thing* for which she personally selected the Metisse contribution. Metisse's debut album has been licensed in many countries, including Japan and France, and they sum up their musical philosophy by saying "We love what we do and we hope we can inspire others or even simply brighten the day with our music". Anyone who has enjoyed their music will know how well they succeed on both fronts.

" My father was the organist with the showband The Bluebell Quartet. They played gigs four nights a week all over the west of Ireland. He would rarely bring the organ home, but I remember vividly the joy of waking up and knowing that it was in the house from the smell of cigarettes and beer that magically wafted from it! According to my parents, I would sit just playing three notes. I found it so interesting that I'd play the same three notes over and over for days!! (Now that I think back, that might explain why the organ was so rarely brought home!) Both my parents are musical, and I seem to have learned every nursery rhyme known to mankind, and I have a fair repertoire of hymns for an atheist. That's my mother's doing.

There was a record player in the house, but we seldom listened to the few records in the family collection. The radio was a far bigger influence on my musical development. The DJ Dave Fanning was the driving force for almost all musicians of my generation. With my first group Real Mayonnaise, our sole goal was to get played on Dave's radio programme on 2FM. We thought we had become mega-gods the day our single 'Framework' was played on his show.

The first gig I went to would have been my father playing with the Bluebell Quartet at the convent in Bandon in County Cork. For a small boy, seeing my father performing on stage probably sowed the seeds of my own musical ambition. The first gig I played as a musician myself was with the band Real Mayonnaise. I think we had five songs that we somehow managed to drag out for an hour at the famous Sir Henry's venue in the Grand Parade Hotel in Cork. I remember one plan was to play a long whiney noise as an intro to a drum fill. But after about five minutes we had to stop to ask the bouncers to allow our drummer to come in. He'd been stopped at the door for being under the age limit!

I became frustrated with the music industry after my second band, The Chapter House, seemed to do everything right, yet it was just not working out career-wise and I couldn't figure out why. So I gave up music totally, and went off to teach

English in France. I absolutely hated it. I can still remember that I used to pass a gardener every morning on my way to work, and again in the evening on my way home, and I felt serious pangs of jealousy comparing the job I had to do for a living with his job. Frustrations for a musician can be terrible, especially when contracts, law and corporate business take over from the music.

On the other hand, I've had some great moments in music. I got a great buzz when Metisse played in front of 100,000 people at the O2 concert in the Phoenix Park in Dublin, and the crowd sang our song 'Boom Boom Ba' along with us!!' "

FAVOURITE SONG: Allegri's 'Miserere' is my favourite song because it's subtle enough, long enough and complex enough to stay interesting even after thousands of listens. Allegri was a sixteenth-century composer born in Rome.

FAVOURITE ARTISTS: The German band, Kraftwerk, for being 30 years ahead of their time and the fathers of electronic music.

FAVOURITE ALBUM: *Leftism* by LeftField, a groundbreaking album that pushed electronic music to the limit.

50

MICK HANLY

Born in Limerick, Mick Hanly is one of Ireland's foremost singer songwriters, with a string of highly successful and beautifully crafted songs to his name. Initially inspired by 1950s rock'n'roll before he was seduced by folk music in the 1960s, Mick has over the years played with numerous groups, including the legendary Moving Hearts. His songs have been covered by various singers from Mary Black and Christy Moore to American country singer Hal Ketchum. Hal took Hanly's 'Past The Point Of Rescue' into the Top 10 of the US country chart in 1993 and earned a coveted Gold Disc for both performer and writer. Hanly now lives in Thomastown, Co Kilkenny.

❝My parents weren't exactly a musical influence. My father was a good tenor singer and had an extensive repertoire of John McCormack-style songs, and there was a lot of singing around the house. My grandmother had snatches of songs that she used to sing to us as children. I heard her sing these to my younger brother and sister when they were suffering from colic. One tune went 'Sackada doadle oh, sackada doadle andy, sackada doadle oh, Seanie is fond of his pandy' (i.e. potatoes and milk). Another went: 'As I went over blackwater, blackwater went over me. I saw two little black-birds perching on a tree. One of them called me a robber, the other one called me a thief. I took out my little blackthorn stick and hit him across the cheek.' I recorded this snatch on an album called *As I Went Over Blackwater* for Mulligan Records in the late seventies. As the piece was so short I asked Declan Sinnott to play slide guitar around the melody, and I have to say it's one of the highlights of the album for me.

Radio was a huge influence in my early years, Radio Luxembourg in particular. I remember hearing ' I Wanna Be Your Man' by the Rolling Stones and 'Love Me Do' by The Beatles on radio for the first time and being totally blown away by them. I also heard the instrumental 'Apache' by The Shadows and wanted to make that sound. I was quite dis-appointed that the guitar that had been bought for my brother for £2:10 shillings, and which got me started on the instrument, didn't quite reproduce the Hank Marvin sound! I listened to the DJ Alan Freeman every Sunday for two hours when the Merseybeat boom was in full swing. The Hollies, The Animals, The Spencer Davis Group and Andy Fairweather Low, with his group Amen Corner, were particular favourites. I later saw Andy live in the Jetland Ballroom in Limerick. That was a big thrill.

I can't pinpoint the first real gig I was at, but there were lots of bands playing the Cavalier Club in Limerick, including The People and The Creatures, with fine individual musicians like Peter Adler and Fran O'Toole. I wasn't all that impressed with some of the 'longhairs' at the time, but Henry McCullough was hugely impressive, as was Johnny Duhan of Granny's Intentions. My first real gig was probably one of those. I saw

Phil Lynott and Them (but without Van Morrison) in the Franciscan Hall. There was usually a Franciscan at each side of the stage to keep tabs on the heavy petters. They were our equivalent of the Hell's Angels at Altamont, but with different gear and a different set of values.

I spent two years in the ESB and loathed the work, but I liked some of the people there. I never chose to be a professional musician. I kinda drifted into it through my love of playing the guitar, my shyness, and the possibility of a free lunch. Unfortunately, there turned out to be no free lunch. There's a lot of freedom in being your own boss, but if you want to produce anything of any value you must have a lot of discipline. The same old clichés apply to life as a musician; you get out only what you put in.

One of the best moments in music for me personally was writing 'Past The Point Of Rescue'. It has allowed me the freedom to write the songs that I want to write, so I have to be grateful for that moment of inspiration. Had it not been a success, I would be a fairly handy forklift driver by now!

For the modicum of talent that I have, I feel that I've done very well in the music business. There are times when I feel it would be nice if someone said 'Here, there's fifty grand. Go and make a record'. But then they might demand a say in the contents and what might they know about my music? Nothing, probably. Most of the movers and shakers in the music business know a lot about figures, but their ears are painted on."

FAVOURITE SONGS: I hear all of Van Morrison's album, *Astral Weeks,* as one song and it's my favourite. After that the list is endless, but I'll go for 'Stardust'.

FAVOURITE SONGWRITERS: Randy Newman, Yip Harburg, Joni Mitchell, Rodgers and Hart, Cole Porter, Hank Williams.

FAVOURITE ALBUMS: *Sail Away* by Randy Newman, *Blood On The Tracks* by Bob Dylan, *Blue* by Joni Mitchell, *Redheaded Stranger* by Willie Nelson, the Planxty albums, Emmylou Harris' *Pieces Of The Sky*. They all wear the years so well.

51

MIKE HANRAHAN

Reared in Ennis in Co Clare, Mike Hanrahan has been involved in the music business as a singer, songwriter and guitarist since the late seventies, starting his professional career with a band called Tumbleweed. In 1980 he joined Stockton's Wing for whom he wrote several songs, including their hits 'Beautiful Affair' and 'Walk Away'. The band were critically acclaimed worldwide for their eclectic blend of traditional and contemporary Irish music, using electric and acoustic instruments. Mike left the band in 1984 to pursue his solo ambitions and since then has enjoyed further success as a solo artist, in 2002 releasing a well-received album called *What You Know*.

❝ One of my earliest musical memories is writing a hymn as part of a school project when I was about twelve in sixth class. But then I'd been born into a veritable bubble of music. We always had music at home. There were eight of us in the house and every one of us played an instrument. My parents loved music. My grand-mother played the concertina and my grandfather on my mother's side played the accordion. I learned to play tin whistle at school too. It skipped a generation and landed on me! I used to sing, and we had a band as young kids called the St Michael's Ceili Band after the place we were reared in, St Michael's in Ennis. We entered *fleadhs* and *feis ceoils*, but we also played in many local places, doing local charity gigs or whatever came up.

I vividly remember us getting our first record player. They were big awkward things in those days. My dad bought a selection of records, including classical music like the Strauss waltz *The Blue Danube*. We had Rolf Harris and The Dubliners' albums, and, believe it or not, the Rolling Stones were in there too. That was a measure of my life then. My older brother was very much into modern music and he used to listen to Radio Caroline and Radio Luxembourg which broadcast the pop and rock music of the day. He used to buy albums from Cog Records, a mail order company based in Wales. So at a very early age I listened to progressive rock bands like Gentle Giant and Van Der Graaf Generator.

My dad used to work in a dance-hall, so I went to a lot of gigs and concerts and dances. I saw almost every single band that came to town, including the Dubliners. I remember seeing Butch Moore perform when I was about eight or nine. He was the first singer to represent Ireland in the Eurovision Song Contest with a song called 'Walking The Streets In The Rain'. I remember having my photograph taken with him.

I was mad into the showbands when I was a child, and I used to collect the photographs of the various bands which they'd give out at the shows. They were the bands who made me feel I wanted to be up there on the stage. We were reared on the showbands and there were some great bands around. The Royal Showband with Brendan Bowyer were an incredible live act. The guys in those bands were serious players.

So from as far back as I can remember, all I've ever wanted to be was a musician. As I moved through my teens I wanted to be a writer too. My biggest problem was figuring out how I was going to do it, because in my town the tradition was to leave school, get a secure job and settle down in time and raise a family. After I got a job in Shannon Airport my constant worry was, "How am I going to get out of this routine and get on the road with my music"?

My biggest influence musically was Leonard Cohen. At thirteen I heard his records, bought a book of his songs and learned how to play guitar from a tutor book called *Finger Picking*. I was drawn to Cohen's lyrics and his voice. He's a very clever writer, a great man with his words which are so measured. His guitar playing was kind of special, and I lived and breathed Leonard Cohen for many years, and no doubt bored many with his albums over the years too.

In 1982 Stockton's Wing were playing regular pub and club gigs, and when the single 'Beautiful Affair' broke it introduced us to an audience which hadn't known us before. Up to that point we had a cult following, but the radio brought us a much younger audience. So the average age at our gigs dropped as we drew more people. We started making a few bob and attracted attention beyond Ireland, with tours of the UK and the festival circuits of Europe and America. So that single was a turning point as it was quite unusual for what was regarded as a traditional band to be writing pop songs.

I like being busy. I'm an active person, and that's how I

survive. A few years ago my father's death had a profound effect on my life. This might sound strange, but it gave me the kick in the arse to start writing again. His death was a pivotal event in my life and in my music career.

People ask me why I write songs and expose my innermost feelings to other people. I believe that the better you get at songwriting the better you can share those private moments in your life with somebody else. That's the magic of it. When I'm sitting at home, thinking about writing a song and along comes a really good idea, that is a magic, magic moment for me. Later, you share it with the musicians who record it with you and then you share it with the audience. It all starts with that bit of an idea.

But you don't always have to be detailed about personal things. I think you can be very clever and exorcise your own demons without really imposing on anyone. But what you're hoping to do is touch people who listen to your work, who connect on that level. That's the beauty of writing. It's like when you read a book and you think, "I'd love to have written that book", because it has touched you in some way. That's why I write, to share my feelings and emotions with whoever wants to connect with them."

52

MOYA BRENNAN

Born in Donegal in 1952, Moya Brennan (Máire Ní Bhraonáin as Gaeilge) has been part of the group Clannad for nearly thirty years during which they adventurously blended the old with the new in a style that is uniquely their own. A highly accomplished harp player and lead singer with the internationally-acclaimed group, Moya has enjoyed enormous success both with Clannad and through her many solo projects, including the 'Theme from 'Harry's Game', the BAFTA award-winning soundtrack for the film, *Robin of Sherwood*, a Grammy for their album, *Landmarks*, and her hit duet with Bono 'In A Lifetime'. While Clannad's influence can be heard across a wide spectrum of music from *Riverdance* to the *Titanic* soundtrack, their appeal crosses all generations too, and they have even become darlings of the dance-floor, thanks to a recent collaboration with Chicane on the Top 10 hit 'Saltwater'. They are currently working on a live album for release later this year.

"My most vivid memory of music when I was younger is of my mum teaching old Gaelic songs for the local *feis* and singing with my sisters late at night. We used to share a room in our home in Donegal and singing in bed would always help us get to sleep.

We didn't have a radio in our house until I was about fourteen or fifteen. It was then that I discovered the pirate stations, particularly Radio Caroline. Hearing the Beach Boys and Mamas and Papas had a huge influence on the kind of harmonies Clannad would later specialise in.

My parents had a musical background, very much so. Most of my relations seemed to be involved in music to some extent. My mother was a music teacher and my father was the leader of his own Showband (the Slieve Foy), which included his sister and brother as well as my mother, until the seventies when he bought a pub called Leo's Tavern where he still performs to this day. In fact Clannad started out by playing gigs in Leo's. Through our first gigs in Leo's Tavern we gained experience and confidence and at our first show elsewhere, at the Letterkenny Folk Festival, we entered a competition and won first prize!

The first gig I went to was one given by the Breton harpist, Alan Stivell, at the RDS. He was very popular in Ireland throughout the seventies and he must have been a big influence on my harp playing.

Somehow I always knew that I would do something in music - although if I'd thought about it I would probably have thought it might be as a music teacher. I never really imagined that Clannad could become a career, or that I would be able to support myself financially as a full-time musician.

I've been asked to pick the best moment in my music career so far, but there have to be several moments that stand out. Winning the Letterkenny Folk Festival was obviously a great break for us and a major boost to our confidence. Winning a BAFTA award for the soundtrack of the film, *Robin of Sherwood*, was another, as was the Grammy award for the album, *Landmarks*.

There have also been a number of memorable concerts around the world, like playing the Royal Albert Hall, the Philharmonic Hall in Berlin and performing in front of 2.7 million people (including the Pope) in Rome.

Although we've had to work incredibly hard at times, I can't say I've ever felt frustrated enough to want to get out of the music business. Of course the business has its ups and downs, but being in a family band has held us together over the years. We've never toured so extensively that it has ever become unbearable."

FAVOURITE SONG: 'The Circle Game' by Joni Mitchell

FAVOURITE ARTIST: Joni Mitchell

FAVOURITE ALBUM: *Ladies of the Canyon* by Joni Mitchell

53

MUNDY

Mundy was born in Birr, Co Offaly. After a spell signed to Sony Music, his self-penned and self-financed album, *24 Star Hotel*, became a significant commercial hit in 2002. That album was his much-anticipated follow up to *Jellylegs*, which had catapulted the Offaly singer onto the international stage in late 1996. Its success saw the then 20-year-old Mundy tour with international stars of the calibre of Alanis Morrisette, Neil Young, Van Morrison and The Manic Street Preachers among others. Further success came Mundy's way when his song 'To You I Bestow' featured on the soundtrack to Baz Luhrmann's film, *Romeo and Juliet*, which went on to sell a staggering 11 million copies worldwide. Mundy is renowned for his vibrant live performances, which have seen him grace countless stages across Europe and further afield. Still only 26, he has covered more ground than most, and yet in some many ways one suspects that this talented man's journey is only just beginning.

"My first musical memory goes back to me getting my very first guitar when I was only five. I became really excited by music through regular visits to my aunt's house in Portlaoise and listening to her records, which would have included the Royal Showband with their singer Brendan Bowyer and their big Irish hit 'The Hucklebuck', and stuff like that. That's also how I became familiar with the fifties rock'n'roller Bill Haley and the Comets. That was when I first got really excited about music. It appealed to me because I had nothing to compare it to. It was the first music I heard, and everything else after that actually seemed quite boring by comparison. To my innocent ears this music seemed to be alive, and when someone put the vinyl on the record player all the aunts and uncles in the house would start dancing.

I had four different ambitions that I wanted to achieve when I was growing up. First of all, I wanted to swim for Ireland, be an Olympic swimmer. The second goal I had was to be something like a showjumper. I also wanted to hurl for Offaly (of course) and my last desire was to be a musician. They were the four stages that got me to where I am today. I achieved some of those ambitions too. I swam for Offaly twice, I did racing and showjumping and won some rosettes for that. In fact, I've got a few hurling medals for playing for Birr, my home-town.

But I always kept up my musical interests, so when I was around fourteen I attempted to play the guitar properly and started to listen to Bob Dylan and the likes, and I just gave up the outdoor sporting activity for the more attractive indoor version. To be quite honest, I still dream about the others, but with music there is something marvellous about being able to put thoughts on paper and use it to get a lot of stuff out of your system. It's also a great way of being able to relate to other people and to share your joy and sadness with them.

The first records I got were by the blues artist, Muddy

Waters, singer-songwriter Neil Young, The Doors from the sixties and the more contemporary REM. These first few albums were so impressive they nearly lifted my head off.

For me the biggest achievement with my own music is the writing of new songs. There is nothing that makes me happier than coming up with a new idea or a new song. When an audience later sings that same song back to you, it's a very beautiful and self-gratifying moment. I wrote a song called 'July' which became a bit of a summer hit back in 2002, and I performed this song in front of a few thousand people at the Witnness festival a few months later. When they sang that song back to me, it genuinely brought a tear to my eye with the joy of hearing all those voices singing my song. It's unbelievable when you get a response like that, because I was once told that my songs weren't really very good and I lost my record deal with Sony Music over all that stuff. So when you go out there onto that stage and you fight your corner and five or six thousand people are singing along to your song it's like winning a very important battle.

My friends have been the biggest influences on my life. I have some friends who have certain powers and certain skills and I take an awful lot of leaves out of their books. There's not just one person who keeps me going, it's a lot of people, and I owe a lot of thanks to all of them. Right now I'm happier than I've been in years. I call my own shots, I can say 'yes' or 'no' to whomever I want and the songs are either good or bad."

FAVOURITE SONG: 'Skylarkin' by Mic Christopher

FAVOURITE SINGER: Roy Orbison

54

NAIMEE COLEMAN

Naimee Coleman was born in 1977. At the tender age of eighteen she signed her first record deal and year after year her music career has moved consistently upwards and onwards. First discovered singing backing vocals for a local Dublin band, Naimee released her debut album *Silver Wrists* in 1997, selling in excess of 50,000 copies. Four busy years later she followed with her second album *Bring Down The Moon* while also gaining worldwide recognition with a UK Top 5 hit with Aurora's dance version of Duran Duran's 'Ordinary World'.

*"*My earliest childhood memory of music is a mixture of Julie Andrews in *The Sound of Music* and The Beatles. That combination might seem like a weird one, but growing up it was a major influence. I remember very clearly being in the senior infants class in school and being very lucky that our teacher taught the class Beatles songs instead of the usual curriculum songs. We were learning songs like 'Good Day, Sunshine' and several other songs from the Beatles' *Revolver*

album. The teacher took a shine to me because I responded to the songs. He used to give a lot of his time to teaching me the music, so I got so excited about this band called The Beatles that my mother rooted out all her old Beatles albums and my fascination with music really started from there.

I always wanted to be a musician, and that's one thing I've always been thankful for. That ambition was always there in my mind and I was very lucky going all the way through primary school to have amazing teachers who always encouraged me to sing. I believe that really helped me. Perhaps if that hadn't happened my mind might have begun to think about other things and my musical interests might have been squashed down by day-to-day life. Fortunately it never happened.

Our house when I was a child was always full of music. Both my parents were very musical and were young enough to buy lots of records and to play music, so there was always music around in one form or the other. I did my piano lessons and my choir practice as well, and those two different forms of music-making helped me too.

My parents regularly bought me the *Now That's What I Call Music* LP compilations so I had a terrific collection of songs to listen to. I remember hearing Katrina and the Waves' 'Walking on Sunshine' and getting really excited about that song and deciding there and then that I wanted to be in a band. I used to dance around the front room frantically to that record. *Top of the Pops* on television was another big influence. I thought it was great. I used to watch it sometimes just to see what people were wearing more than anything else, because it was just so glamorous and so exciting. I don't think my parents were into the programme at all. They were a bit too 'cool' for it, but I loved it.

Although I had always wanted to sing I don't think I had

ever thought it through in practical terms. But just to imagine I could be in a band, with drums and everything, and to be able to have people dance to my songs inspired me in the right direction.

The very first time I recorded in a proper recording studio was when I was fourteen. I got the chance through a favour. I had written a song with a friend whose brother just happened to work in Sun Studios in Temple Bar in Dublin, and he got us in there really late one night. It was very cheap to record your demo at night, but we made a god-awful racket. But while I was doing it I got a great buzz, singing into the mike, putting on the headphones and doing the whole thing. I really thought that this was something special!

When I played my first gig aged sixteen I kind of realised that this was something I could do with confidence and that I would like to do it over and over and over again. Those two memories, the recording and the live gig, sealed it for me.

The American singer-songwriter, Suzanne Vega, was a big influence on me. The first single I ever bought after saving up my pocket money was 'Luka' by Suzanne Vega. I bought the 12" version and I used to play it to death. Ever since then I have loved her work– she's an incredible musician. My mum had most of Joni Mitchell's albums and I used to sit singing along to her stuff. It was great to be able to listen to quality music like that.

As a teenager I was seriously into Pearl Jam and Guns'n'Roses and Metallica. I was a real oul' rocker! I don't think any of that type of music has necessarily transferred into my own music *per se*, but that was the kind of music I was into at the time. But when I turned eighteen I started listening to many more of the female singer-songwriters such as Sarah McLachlan, Ani DiFranco, Aimee Mann and Paula Cole. They have all inspired me.

I'm very happy with my lot today. I've been incredibly lucky in my work and I've had the most amazing opportunities. I got to appear on *Top of the Pops* and all sorts of other programmes. But now I've reached the stage where I'm writing material for my next album while also looking at my long-term desire to make albums without worrying too much about having the commercial success. That kind of success would have been a bit more important to me in the past. Now I'm far more interested in making a quality album that might still sound good in ten years' time, something with a bit of longevity to it. I know it's easier said than done, but that's where my head is at at the moment."

FAVOURITE SINGERS: Suzanne Vega and Ani DiFranco.

FAVOURITE SONG: 'Let's Stay Together' by Al Green

BIGGEST INFLUENCE: The Beatles

FAVOURITE ALBUM: *The Beatles*. (the "white album")

IRISH ARTIST THAT I LOOK UP TO:
Glen Hansard (The Frames)

55

PADDY COLE

Paddy Cole, a native of County Monaghan, is an internationally acclaimed sax and clarinet player. Known as Ireland's very own "King of Swing", his career as a professional musician spans over thirty years. Rising to prominence during the era when showbands majestically ruled the Irish music scene, Paddy was a key member of the now legendary Capitol Showband and then reached even dizzier heights with the Big Eight Showband with whom he toured across the US and played to huge crowds in Las Vegas as one of the resort's most popular resident bands. Paddy's enthusiasm for music has never wavered and he continues to play at jazz festivals around the world.

❞One of the memories of music that has stayed with me from an early age is of my father. He used to have a music tutor book and he would take me through a chapter of it at a time to teach me the basics of music on the saxophone. When he came home every evening he would check me out to see if I could play the latest exercise he'd given me. So when I came home from school each day I'd go in to blowing the sax for practice, while I could hear the other boys in the field at the back of our house playing football. At that stage I used to hate the music. But then I developed a love for it myself over time and I became self-taught on the clarinet. Although my father never played that particular instrument, there was an old clarinet in the house and I used to be blowing at it every now and then, and I developed a deep liking for jazz music and it went on from there.

I remember going to a concert in Castleblaney in County Monaghan where my father was playing with the Regal Showband. It was a concert, not a dance as was more common for showbands in those days. He played a very difficult piece for a saxophone, a piece called 'Saxophobia'. If you could play that piece you were accepted as a really top-class sax player. I remember being very proud of him as I sat there listening to him play it. I was only seven or eight years old at the time, but I can remember it as if it was only yesterday.

When I think back to the first gig that I played at as a musician, the first thing I remember is that I was so nervous that when I stood up to play a solo piece on my own, nothing happened! I was so nervous I couldn't get a note out. My father was playing behind me, and he took the tune and started it off until eventually when it got going I was able to join in. My father was a huge influence on me and he genuinely loved to see me getting on in the music business. In actual fact, when I was first offered the job in the Capitol Showband, my mother wasn't very keen on me moving from Monaghan to live in Dublin to be nearer the band business. But my father was very keen for me to do it because he wanted to see me succeed in the music business.

I found it a huge change when I later went to America. We had done several tours of America with the Capitol Showband. There were huge ballrooms in New York, Chicago, Boston,

Philadelphia and San Francisco. We used to go on tours regularly, and even went up to Canada. But when I went to live in Las Vegas for the six or seven months of the year it was brilliant altogether!

We were doing our own gigs, which were pretty tough. We were doing three shows a night, six nights a week. But we got to see and hear a lot of the top acts, like Elvis Presley, Frank Sinatra and acts of that calibre. We'd get to see them live several times. Memories like that cannot be bought. I remember once being in the dressing-room with Elvis. He was a really nice guy. The one thing I always remember about him was that he was so tall. We have wonderful memories, happy memories of happy days in the music business.

We had a family bar and restaurant in Castleblaney at that time, so when I came back from Las Vegas I was running it. But I also used to run Monday night jazz sessions too. They were hugely popular in the bar, but I still went and played cabaret spots in Clontarf Castle on the northside of Dublin and in the Braemore Rooms out in Churchtown on the southside.

I suppose Twink was instrumental in encouraging me to get fired up again about going full-time when I got back to Ireland. She got me spots on a couple of shows, including talking me into doing a couple of shows in Clontarf Castle with her. So eventually the decision was made to sell the pub and get back into music full-time. I always went to the Cork Jazz Festival, even when I had the pub, and I'd sit in and play with different bands, so you could in a way say that I never lost my love for music. At every stage, one way or the other, I was involved in the band business.

I've been asked so many times what my best moment in music has been. One of the candidates would have to be when I received the Hall of Fame award at the National Concert Hall. That was a huge milestone in my career in the business. All in all I've had a very good life through music, and I wouldn't wish to change any of it."

FAVOURITE ALBUM: Anything by the New Orleans jazz trumpeter, Louis Prima

FAVOURITE SONG: 'MacArthur Park' sung by Richard Harris

56

PADDY
MOLONEY
THE CHIEFTAINS

Paddy Moloney is a founding member of one of the most famous traditional Irish acts ever. The Chieftains evolved in the early sixties from the group Ceoltoiri Chualann. The band has survived over four decades and become acknowledged as Ireland's most internationally recognised traditional music group. As a virtuoso piper, inventive arranger and charismatic leader of the band, Moloney has had a significant input into the group's success. His exceptional skills as a musician have helped The Chieftains sell millions of albums across the world and accumulate numerous awards, including coveted Grammies. The band has successfully collaborated with many legendary musicians from several genres of music, from a Chinese orchestra to Van Morrison, Paul McCartney, Art Garfunkel, Sting, Jackson Browne and Emmylou Harris. Moloney and his band have been among the foremost musical ambassadors for both Ireland and for traditional music.

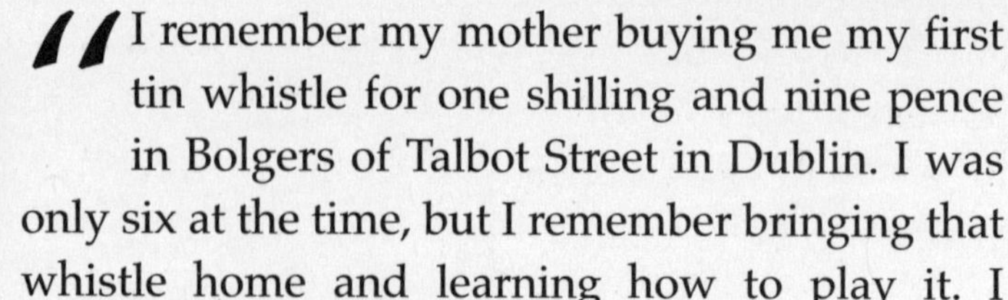

I remember my mother buying me my first tin whistle for one shilling and nine pence in Bolgers of Talbot Street in Dublin. I was only six at the time, but I remember bringing that whistle home and learning how to play it. I moved on to learning the uilleann pipes when I was about eight or nine. The late Leo Rowsome, 'The King Of The Pipers' as he was called, taught me. There used to be an area in 'the hollow' in the Phoenix Park and in those days I remember during the summertime, sitting up there with all the other young pipers to play for the people. My two legs would be hanging down, gangling (as you might know I'm not very tall) and I was quite small at the time in my short trousers. Just playing for all those people was a great sensation. Those were great times for a musician.

I've had a hell of life, thank God! I have been given a gift from God, helping people to enjoy listening to music, making them happy, joyful or sad as the case might be, and I've got super satisfaction from that in the past and still do to this very day. During a recent concert in the USA in the Lincoln Center on Saint Patrick's night, the crowd made it feel like there were about forty-two of us on stage. It was such a truly wonderful occasion.

As I was growing up I couldn't get enough music. I was always on to my ma to bring me to hear music all over the place. I was also very lucky in that I had great musical neighbours around the Donnycarney area on the north side of Dublin. The great Leo Rowsome was up the street, Danny Dowd was around the corner, there were Peter Flynn and Jack Lynch, and another man called Lynch who had a band going in Marino School. They were great times. I loved going to people's houses, sitting and playing music, trying out tunes. Unfortunately I was so tied up in the music that I was not studying enough, I'm sorry to say! I was meant to be going to be an accountant at one stage. My mother had that in mind for me, but I got to the stage where the music took over completely and I only got half way with my accountancy studies. I might be doing grand up to Christmas and then the parties would start and so would the music sessions and the studies would stop!

But later I put the music to good use and made a career out of it instead. Before that happened I was on the management staff of Baxendales, a builders' providers in Capel Street in Dublin. I then worked with Claddagh Records for eight years, and that got me deeply involved in the whole music industry. It was fascinating, and the music industry has brought me tremendous opportunities and I've had a great innings.

I started the band in November of 1962, although it was beginning to come together for me back in the mid-fifties. I had various combinations, groups and various line-ups, and was always experimenting, as I do to this very day, always looking for new adventures and new challenges. Music has been my life, every day of it; I just love it and still do.

I think The Chieftains were a challenge from the start. It took many a year to really build it up, and there were several years of a gap between getting the first album out and the appearance of the second one in 1969. But it was getting bigger and the renowned DJ John Peel in England was playing our music and some of the Rolling Stones were coming to our concerts. So there was an obvious interest in what we were doing, and it wasn't restricted to folk fans either. We were doing it our way, as the Song goes, and we continued to do that until we could consider that playing in the band could become a full-time job. That's never an easy decision for any musician to take, especially with families to think of. It was a big undertaking for us, but to me we had a particularly special sound and now The

Chieftains are well established to the point where you could say we've become an institution.

I've had many of my dreams come true and I have some fantastic memories. 27 years ago I told the newspapers that if I got the chance I would have loved to be the first person to play his own instrument live on the moon. But my son, just by coincidence, is now working for NASA in Houston, Texas! So over the last four or five years I've been able to meet up with the astronauts and talk to them. They have never ruled that dream out to this day, so you never know. There's always the possibility that I'll fulfil that dream!! An astronaut by the name of Katie Coleman comes to our concerts. She plays the flute with a group called The Astronautics and she brought one of my tin whistles up to space with her, along with some of our tapes. She later presented my whistle back to me in a glass case. So it's been around the world a fair few times!

Looking to the future, I always have new ideas about different things I'd like to explore. Our record company wasn't satisfied with all the albums they got since they signed us in 1985, so they want another five from us! So I've got to get on my bicycle and keep things really moving up to 2005, with various recordings to be done and places to go and ideas to fulfil. The first forty-one years of The Chieftains have been great, but I have personal ambitions to get on with as well. So I need to pace myself a bit better; I wish there were forty-eight hours in every day!"

57

PAUL BRADY

Paul Brady has been a dominant force on the Irish music scene for decades. After an early career that spanned rock music with The Kult and folk music with The Johnstons, he became a key member of Planxty, joining one of the most influential Irish trad bands of all time in 1974. As a songwriter he has had his songs covered by artists as diverse as Tina Turner, David Crosby, Bonnie Raitt and Santana. He has worked with some of the top artists around, including Mark Knopfler and Ronan Keating. He has also earned the public acclaim of rock legends of the calibre of Bob Dylan and Eric Clapton.

❝Our family in Strabane had a strong sense of the Irish musical tradition. My father's mother was a fine singer and pianist who won prizes at the Sligo *Feis*. My father was a gifted performer and singer, taking part in local drama societies and producing shows. My mother had grown up in a family of small farmers with a leaning towards traditional music in rural Fermanagh and her brother was a fiddle player. When we went as a family to Bundoran in County Donegal for our holidays we used to visit singing hotels at night and my father was a regular performer at those. I also listened to the radio a lot, but despite the presence of music all around me I don't think there was anything that would have suggested I'd make a career out of it.

I moved to Dublin to attend university when I was seventeen. I'd led a comparatively localised life until then, never having ventured much further than Tyrone, Donegal, or Derry where I'd attended boarding school. Sixties Dublin was a whole new experience for me. Until then, I'd been hearing music in my head and in my own living room, but the opportunity to see live groups (as we called them then), performing music other than showband material was really exhilarating. I can recall a show at the Crystal Ballroom, which later became McGonagles, with four bands on the bill, Bluesville, The Inmates, The Greenbeats and The Semi-Tones. Seeing soul, rhythm and blues and rock music live right before my eyes was like dying and going to heaven. I'd bought an electric guitar when I was in Tyrone, so I joined The Inmates as rhythm guitarist and vocalist before we became The Kult.

By the mid-sixties there was an explosion of what we called beat clubs around Dublin. There was Sound City on Burgh Quay, The Carousel in Glasthule, the Five Club in Harcourt Street, and The Cavalier. Rugby and tennis clubs also ran hops (dances), which used live bands. There could have been over fifty really good bands in Dublin at the time, including Philip Lynott in The Black Eagles, and The Gnumphs, but they mostly did non-original songs.

Across the street from the Five Club was the Ninety-Five Club, which specialised in trad, folk and blues. I often went there as a fan, but when I began to play solo blues and folk songs I played gigs there as well.

In 1967 I joined The Johnstons, and that was the start of about fifteen years spent on the folk scene, joining Planxty and playing and recording with Andy Irvine. I think I decided that music was what I wanted as a career during my time with The Johnstons who moved from the purely traditional world into contemporary folk, singing songs by Leonard Cohen, Gordon Lightfoot, Ewan McColl, Jacques Brel, Joni Mitchell, and releasing two albums on the same day, one contemporary and one traditional.

So even then I was interested in different kinds of music. I began to write songs, like 'Brightness She Came', 'You Oughta Know', 'Continental Trailways Bus' and 'December Windows'. I wanted to be a songwriter then, but my career took a different direction through events I had little control over. For instance, after being in New York for a few years I was invited to join Planxty after Christy Moore left. The Johnstons had just broken up and I couldn't get a record deal. I was partly grabbing at a lifeline, although I was excited by the thought of working with Donal Lunny and Andy Irvine, as I admired both. They too were into Woody Guthrie and the blues, and when I had attended Art College I had gigged with Donal.

Moving back into rock music later was a risk, but most things I've done in my career have been a bit risky, although I crave security in a way. I've never seen myself as just an entertainer, but as someone given the gift of getting to the core of different types of songs. I've also accepted the fact that there has to be some notion of marketing or style. But it's something I've never wanted to confront, and my choices were usually based on the music.

Assuming that my songs are autobiographical is going too far, but I use a trick I learned from my father's monologues. He would tell a story that hadn't happened to him, yet it seemed like it had. So the lyrics of, say, 'Nothing But The Same Old Story' didn't all happen in my life. But I lived in London with a bit of a ghetto Irish outlook, so I could relate to what happened to the character in the song.

I was tempted to give up music as a career in the nineties. After my album, *Spirits Colliding,* I co-wrote with artists all over the world and it was extremely enjoyable. I was becoming tired of the music business after my long-term relationship with my manager Paul Cummins ended. That was a traumatic experience and left a sour taste for some time. My record deal with Mercury Records also ended. I had no sense of achievement and it seemed like too much hard work, spending maybe two years writing songs, another year recording them and then another year promoting the album. But in the late nineties I realised that I would always want to write, perform and record music. I'd never stopped to appreciate what I'd done over the years but had struggled to justify myself. So I decided to make records and release them without any high expectations. From then on I felt I didn't have to prove anything, not even to myself.

I've never experienced anything but grief from the A&R departments of the record companies I've dealt with. The cost of gaining their support is usually to give up who you are and become what they want you to be. A&R people seem to regard the artist as an extension of their own ambitions. The music business is not concerned with making music, but selling it. But nowadays you can record your own records and release them yourself. The mystique about record companies has disappeared. If Paul Brady can have his own record company then anybody can!"

58

PHIL COULTER

Born in Derry in February 1942, Phil Coulter is an internationally acclaimed producer, composer and performer, achieving far too many successes to list them all here. Coulter, with his songwriting partner Bill Martin, penned the winner of the 1968 Eurovision Song Contest, 'Puppet on a String', sung by Sandie Shaw, and was runners-up in 1969 with Cliff Richard's 'Congratulations'. Coulter also arranged Dana's 1970 winner, 'All Kinds of Everything'. He penned some of our most enduring songs, including 'Scorn Not His Simplicity' and 'The Town I Love So Well', wrote a succession of hits for the phenomenally 'The Bay City Rollers, and has had his songs interpreted by artists as diverse as Elvis Presley, Luke Kelly and Sinead O'Connor.

" I was fortunate to be brought up in Derry where music was part of the fibre of life. It was everywhere, in our family home and at school. We had music festivals and choirs at the Christian Brothers and Derry has a history of choral societies and choirs as well as popular music. During the war years allied personnel, including the British Navy, British Army and American Air Force, were stationed around Derry, so there was a ready-made demand for bands to play at dances for the troops.

So in my younger days I was aware of the culture of dance bands about Derry, and that transmogrified into showbands during my teenage years. Classical, Irish and popular music were around me all the time. Music in Derry wasn't kept for the concert platform or for church on Sundays or for the *feis ceoil*. It was everywhere, and there was no escaping it! To this day everyone in Derry thinks they can sing, especially at what they call "A Big Night". A big night could be to celebrate an engagement, or a family coming home from abroad or a holiday or whatever. But it would not be a party in Derry unless there was a singsong. It is a point of honour that everybody has a party piece, to play, sing, dance or tell a story, whenever they're asked at such a party.

I was very much attracted by the music thing at an early stage. As far as I can remember, the first time I was galvanised by pop music was during the early rock'n'roll era by acts like Fats Domino and Buddy Holly. I spent hours trying to work out the piano intro to Fats Domino's 'Blueberry Hill' when I was just a kid. That music just fired my imagination. It was burning away inside me when I was practising my scales and learning how to play the piano classically at St Columb's College in Derry where I spent six years. St Columb's was a very academic institution, the only college to produce two Nobel prize-winners, John Hume for Peace and Seamus Heaney for Literature. It also produced people like Brian Friel, Paul Brady, Fergal Sharkey and Eamon McCann, quite an impressive track record.

In the late 40's the Labour government in the United

Kingdom instituted a scholarship system for third-level education. This was a great opportunity for kids from working-class backgrounds like myself to get to university. So in St Columb's it was drummed into us to "keep the head down". If you had the talent you were encouraged to apply yourself to your studies because with the right qualifications you could buy into a lifestyle that nobody in your family could have bought into before. Derry was then a very deprived area, so life was tough, with an unemployment rate running well over 30 per cent. Women went out to work in factories, there was a culture of men on the dole, and I grew up with that. So the idea of getting a secure, pensionable job, like a teacher, a civil servant or a lawyer, was something many people around me aspired to.

I had two passions, music and languages, so when I went to university I did music, French and Celtic studies. My father was a cop, and, believe it or not, during my universities days I actually harboured ambitions to join the Foreign Service. I saw myself as "our man in Havana"! I liked the idea of the white suit and the panama hat. The travelling part intrigued me then, and still does. Fortunately that all came adrift, because I think at university I really discovered myself and found that my number one passion was music. So I started a band in my very first term at university and from then on my fate was sealed.

There were a couple of significant milestones along that early road that pointed me towards a career in music. One was when some bright spark at university dreamed up the idea of making a student record as a fund-raising project for the annual rag week. Making a record was quite unusual in the early- to mid-sixties. But I was the guy who had a band; I was "Mr. Music", so when they came to me I said "great idea". I wrote a couple of songs, got my quartet together and we knocked up the record and released it as a promo for the fund-raiser. To have my own record out and to see my picture on the front of that record certainly pushed me further down the music road. The song was called 'Fooling Time'. The Capital Showband, my heroes of the hour, later recorded it and when I got into the charts with a song sung by Butch Moore and the Capital Showband I thought that was it. As of that moment I became unemployable!

But there was innocence then too. Today there is a very well trodden path for would-be musicians, and a very vibrant music business here in Ireland. Back then there was nothing like that. There were the showbands, of course, but the Irish record industry was in its infancy. I had a couple of songs in the charts in Ireland before I left university. Fortunately I realised that no matter how attractive it might be as a big fish in a small pond, if I really wanted to get anywhere I had to get my ass out of here and into the big league. But there was nobody around to mark my cards or give me a few introductions or tell me what to do or even what not to do. It was very tough at the start, but I was driven.

So I left university on a Friday and got the boat to England the next day. I went straight to knocking on doors in what they used to call Tin Pan Alley, the London streets where most of the music industry companies were based. I had no doubt that this was what I wanted to do and with the conviction, ambition and energy that you have when you're 21 or 22 I didn't see any pitfalls. Depending on your point of view, I was either very courageous or very foolhardy.

I think I played the hand of cards I was dealt very well and I'm quite happy the way it panned out. I would have had a lot to complain about now if I had spent the first twenty years of my working life as a music teacher, hating every minute of it, wanting to be a songwriter and thinking of all the time I would have wasted. I've never had a nine-to-five job. In fact it's more often an 18-hour day! But I don't have any regrets whatsoever.

Whatever decisions I made, right or wrong, I have to live with them. Some choices I made when I might not have been best advised, but I certainly have no complaints at this stage."

FAVOURITE SINGER / ALBUM:
Tom Waits *Heart Attack and Vine*.

FAVOURITE SONG:
There are so many, depending on my mood. I would have to pick a song I wished I'd written. At a push I would pick 'He Ain't Heavy, He's My Brother' written by Bobby Scott and Bobby Russell. Many top artists, from Neil Diamond to the Hollies, have recorded it.

59

PICTUREHOUSE

Dave Browne, lead singer

Born in Dublin, Dave Browne is the lead singer with the Dublin-based band, Picturehouse. Formed in 1989, the group have enjoyed major success at home and abroad, with three proud platinum-selling albums to their name. Renowned for their impassioned live performances across Ireland, Europe and even further afield, Picturehouse have supported various legendary acts such as Meat Loaf and Bon Jovi. They have accumulated many accolades and awards, while their 1999 hit single 'Sunburst' and their 2002 hit 'Everybody Loves My Girl' continue to be among the most played songs on Irish radio.

"Thinking back as far as I can, our house was always full of music. My earliest memory is that my Dad used to have a stereo that was made up of separate parts. When I was really young I used to have to stand on a chair in order to reach up to switch it on. We had Elvis Presley's *40 Greatest Hits* album and I suppose crying at his version of 'Old Shep' is one of the earliest memory I have of music really having a deep effect on me. I couldn't get enough of that music. I loved it even then and I had it on whenever I could.

My mother was a great singer and my dad is big into showing off and singing tunes whenever he gets the chance, so there were always parties and lots of singing going on. I remember being carried down the stairs in our first house in Clondalkin in County Dublin when I was about four. There was a party under way downstairs and I was upstairs in my bed but I really wanted to be part of the party. I just cried until I was brought down to join the carry-on and show off to everybody. I loved that feeling then and I still love that feeling. I think it's just something in you.

When I was growing up I never wanted to be anything else but a singer. I could always sing, but my Dad bought me one of those Casio calculator keyboards so I could learn to play. I played it every chance I got until it couldn't be played any more. I really got a lot of use out of it. My parents noticed my fascination with playing music and so I got a bigger keyboard. I wore that one out too, and two years later I got yet another keyboard, one that you could programme the drums and bass into. That's around the time when I started to write songs. That appealed to me because I could do my own thing with them, and I used to write a song nearly every day. Obviously they were half crap, but the whole point was to write one a day. I never ever doubted, and never ever thought, that I would do anything else ever.

So at some point I got to wanting to be a singer in a band. I was partly driven by innocence and partly by self-belief. I've had a few crappy jobs along the way, but nothing that I wanted to do more than this, write and play music.

The first-ever gig I ever went to was Meat Loaf at Dalymount Park in Dublin in 1981. There's a strange story that goes along with that gig. I was in scout camp and when I came home my mother was playing this new album by Meat Loaf called *Bat Out Of Hell*. The album had been out a few years but she was just getting into it then. She played it for me and I loved it, learning it off verbatim. I did a great Meat Loaf impression and used to make all my friends laugh because I knew the songs inside out. So when he came to play the gig at Dalymount Park my mother got us tickets for the gig. Off we went, saw him sing and thought the whole thing was amazing. But I remember thinking, "I'm going to be up there myself singing on stage someday". Fifteen or sixteen years later Picturehouse supported Meat Loaf at one of his concerts at the Wembley Arena in London and I actually ended up on stage with him! He invited me out to join him and we sang 'Two Out Of Three Ain't Bad' together. That was one of the songs on the *Bat Out Of Hell* album and even today I find it such an amazing thing that my dream could eventually come true like that.

Billy Joel was my biggest musical influence at one point in my career, although not so much any more. I had all his albums and, as far as studying music goes, I knew every single lyric and lick on his records. I thought the way he put his records together was amazing. Some of the songs he has written are just unbelievable. Normally when a person asks you a question like, "Who is your biggest influence?" you try and think of the coolest answer or what would be hip to be into, but at the end of the day there are only a handful of songwriters on the planet as good as Billy Joel and that's the truth, cool or not. He and my parents were my biggest influences.

Many of my dreams came to reality very quickly, like you dream about your song being played on the radio, but that happened to the band very fast. You then dream of a crowd singing your lyrics back to you and that happened very fast. One of the first gigs we ever played was supporting Bon Jovi in the RDS before 36,000 people. We were nervous before we went on stage, but when I was up there the nerves had disappeared. I truly enjoyed myself enormously and I said to myself, "Yep, this is were I want to be. I'm home now". I suppose the dream I have now is to get my music out to as many people as I possibly can all over the world."

FAVOURITE SONG:
It changes as time goes on. At a push, over the last five years, I'd nominate 'The Contender' by Jimmy MacCarthy. Christy Moore did a version of that song on his album and I couldn't stop playing it. It's such an excellent song.

FAVOURITE ALBUM: *Hats* by the Blue Nile.

60

PIERCE TURNER

Having cut his professional music teeth in Ireland with The Arrows Showband, Pierce Turner took himself off to the USA, where he is now domiciled in Manhattan, and from where he makes regular forays to Ireland with his uniquely passionate and unpredictable live shows. Those shows usually feature Turner himself on guitar, vocals and keyboards, but his accompaniment can range from complex backing tapes, a solo fiddle player, a trombonist or a string quartet, to a full rock ensemble. Voted *Hot Press* male artist of the year, he has recorded several albums, including the live *Manana In Manhattan*, *Heaven Is Now*, *Angelic Language* and *Three Minute World*.

" Back in my native Wexford I grew up in a family that was very musical, so there was music all around me from as far back as I can remember. My mother had a dance band and she wrote her own songs, a fact that obviously inspired me to follow that path myself in later life. Wexford being the town in Ireland most associated with opera, I also sang a lot in local operatic productions as well as in the school choir and I participated in the occasional plainchant festival in the area too. But I was fascinated by all kinds of music and sounds, so at the age of nine I joined the HFC Brass and Reed Band.

The problem of buying records was not one that afflicted me as a youth as I borrowed as many records as I could from relations, friends and neighbours, and I had the added advantage that my family had our own record shop in Wexford town. But I think my earliest purchases would probably have included albums such as *Tapestry* by Carole King or *Pet Sounds* by the Beach Boys. I still love the Beach Boys and often do their song 'God Only Knows' as part of my live set. It's one of the few cover versions I've featured regularly over the years.

The first instrument I got was a tin whistle which I had to get for the CBS school band. The first gig I ever went to was to see the Emmet Spiceland in White's Hotel in Wexford. They brought a contemporary touch to traditional music, but they also upset a few people by doing the odd Beatles song as well. I've always liked artists who test the boundaries and go a little against the grain. Their line-up featured Donal Lunny who was later to achieve fame as part of various Irish trad acts including Planxty and Moving Hearts.The first public gig I played for was probably at a local hall run by the CYMS. I played saxophone and sang harmonies."

BIGGEST INFLUENCES: The Beach Boys, Bob Dylan, The Beatles, The Righteous Brothers, and the sixties French singer Françoise Hardy

FAVOURITE SONG: 'God Only Knows' by The Beach Boys

FAVOURITE ALBUM: *Pet Sounds* by The Beach Boys

FAVOURITE SONGWRITER: Bob Dylan

61

RELISH

Emerging from Downpatrick in the mid-90's, Relish are a three-piece mix of black and white, Catholic and Protestant - not that they could care less about skin colour or religious background. Ken Papenfus (guitar, vocals), his brother Carl (drums, vocals) and bass player Darren Campbell were all art-school friends who hooked up together once they realised that all their record collections contained both Curtis Mayfield and Carpenters albums! Their debut album, *Wildflowers*, was a major seller in several countries and spawned the runaway radio hits 'Heart-shaped Box', 'Rainbow Zephyr', 'Let It Fly" and 'You I'm Thinking Of'.

DARREN CAMPBELL

"When I was very young' I can remember sitting and listening to music with my older brother. When he brought new albums home we would listen to them all day. We listened to the radio a lot too; especially the chart shows at the weekend. We would record them and listen to them through the week. I guess this must have had some sort of influence on me, although I did not realise it at the time.

Both my parents had musical backgrounds; my father played the cornet and my mother sang in musicals in England. This is not to say they outwardly encouraged my interest in music. For them, anything else would have been a more suitable career path for me.

Through my teens and early twenties I was more interested in art than music. I wanted to become a graphic designer of some description, so by the end of this phase I was designing album covers. I think I was subconsciously giving a hint to myself. The first gig I ever played at was, I think, in Dublin. It wasn't a great event. I was incredibly nervous and I think it showed. Pinpointing my best moment in music so far is very hard, as I've had so many. Securing a record deal, recording our first album and working with top producers were all big moments.

Perhaps playing with U2 at Slane would be my greatest landmark, an incredible event to be asked to be part of.

Of course there have been times when I have felt frustrated with the music industry. Things don't always go the way we plan them, but I have never felt that I have had enough of this business. Not yet! I don't have a favourite song, or artist, or album, but I probably did when I was younger. I listen to such a broad range of musical genres now. A special time for me is the early 90's American rock scene. It was real and exciting and it definitely had an influence on me musically and personally. Even now I listen to bands like Fishbone, Pixies, Faith No More, Rage Against The Machine and Primus."

KEN PAPENFUS

"Both my parents were medically trained. Mum was a nurse and my dad was a dentist before he became a clinical psychologist. So our house had lots of medical books and encyclopaedias on anatomy and physiology. They fed my curiosity about the human body and when I was very young I wanted to be a doctor. I was surrounded by music all the time, but that seemed to make it fairly ordinary, while I looked at being a doctor as something special. As time passed, music became my priority, as food for the soul became more important than food for the body. This was a very natural and organic development beyond my control.

I can remember Mum and Dad's parties when I was very young, with Dad playing the bongos and Mum singing. These always started with the best intentions but continued on until daylight. My mum was a famous South African jazz singer. She sang in *King Kong,* a famous South African musical, at the Royal Albert Hall in London at the age of twelve. She toured with the Golden City Dixies all over South Africa, landing herself a solo recording deal with EMI Records. She also received the coveted *Miss Entertainment of the Year Award* in 1967.

Her musical career ended when she gave birth to her first son and had to leave South Africa because her husband was a white South African and her son was therefore mixed race. This was deemed illegal under apartheid. Her contemporaries included Miriam Makeba, Hugh Masekela, Dudu Pukwana, Dollar Brand, Chris Gilder and her cousin, drummer and percussionist Louis Moholo of Assagai. He was so hot that Frank Zappa and Weather Report both requested his services.

All the aforementioned left South Africa for flourishing careers in the USA and Europe. On his visit to Cape Town, Brooke Benton turned up at Mum's house unexpectedly and asked her to join him on backing vocals for the Cape Town dates of his South African tour. By a weird twist of fate, Mum had lost her voice and thus lost her ticket to greatness.

My dad, also South African, was famous on the South African music circuit as the only white guy who could play African percussion instruments and teach the black guys a few lessons. He is featured on an album by the once famous Kwela Kids. Suffice it to say that every day of my life has been a musical experience.

Radio was an influence in the sense that it created, and continues to create, a catalogue of memories through the music I hear at different stages of my life. Old ideas, old dreams and old thought processes are instantly reborn when the right record comes on. We can see where we have been and how far we have come. This for me is the great influence of radio. When today I hear, say, David Bowie's 'Space Oddity' or Gladys Knight's 'Midnight Train to Georgia', they recreate a moment in time. This is the great power of the song.

The first gig I went to was when I was still a baby. Mum and Dad were VIP guests at a Percy Sledge gig in either Cape Town or Johannesburg. I have no memory of it other than what I've since been told. The first gig I ever played at was in Belfast as a percussionist. I played the bongos at an event for disabled children. I was in charge of teaching the handicapped kids at the Gateway club how to do some African dance. Subsequently I played and danced to the African background music supplied by Mum and Dad from an album called *Ipi Ntombi*, a famous South African musical.

The biggest thing about my career so far is being able to make the ones I love happy through music. I feel I have given more love to them through music than I could ever put into words. Every day I feel blessed that I can do what I do. Sometimes I feel frustrated too, but frustration can be a wonderful thing as it can often result in a positive break-through to a sense of achievement. It is an indicator of passion and drive, and these are important tools for any artist, and are sometimes a necessary catalyst in the creation of groundbreaking work. The music business is made up of people. It is important to remember this. Corporate companies just have more people than the independents. And just like in any area of life, this industry is made up of good and bad people, so I am very selective about the company I keep.

My favourite songs change by the day. There are so many factors to what makes a favourite song, artist or album at any one moment, but some of those I respect include Prince, D'Angelo, Eminem, The Police, U2, Radiohead and Fishbone. They are artists I can look at today and really believe they want to change the world. They have no fear as artists and deserve to sit alongside Ray Charles, Jimi Hendrix, Bob Dylan, Chuck Berry, The Beatles, The Rolling Stones, Queen, Curtis Mayfield, Nirvana, and the like.

But my biggest influence are those past and present who have shown me and given me unconditional love."

62

RONAN HARDIMAN

In 1990 Ronan Hardiman left his daytime job as a teller with the Bank of Ireland to pursue his dream of one day becoming a respected composer. He quickly became a much sought-after bright new talent within the Irish television and film industry. By 1996, when Michael Flatley commissioned him to compose the music for *Lord Of The Dance*, Hardiman's list of credits was as impressive as they were international, including major commissions from the BBC and Public Broadcasting Service (USA). In March 1998 Hardiman released his first solo CD, *Solas*, which has to date sold over 300,000 copies worldwide.

" It's a family joke that I could play the piano before I could walk. I have vague recollections of being wheeled down to the piano, at around four or five, to whack out things very enthusiastically, much to their entertainment. Later, when I began formal training, I was much more interested in experimentation, picking out tunes from the radio and doodling around for my own amusement, than in learning the formalities and the technical aspects of the piano. Like many musicians I can hear something and play it, and I got through my training that way.

After becoming good on the piano I'd show off to attract attention. But on a trip to Germany when I was eleven or twelve I realised that music could become more than just a casual interest. The family I stayed with had an album I hadn't heard before, *The Beatles 1967-1970*. I got absolutely lost in it, 'Strawberry Fields Forever', 'I Am The Walrus', 'Lucy In The Sky With Diamonds', stuff that even today sounds incredibly fresh. There wasn't an atmosphere of pop culture in our house. The emphasis was more on traditional music and my brothers and sisters went to Irish-speaking schools. So The Beatles were like something from another planet, and I felt differently about music from then on, like a vocation, something I was meant to do by hook or by crook. Music now affected me in a profound way, not just as a chance to show off. From then on, every time I played piano it was to 40,000 people in our sitting room! But I didn't really have the self-confidence to imagine myself having a real career in music.

After taking private piano lessons I took the Royal Irish Academy of Music exams. Some teachers can be conservative and narrow in their view, but I was fortunate in having a teacher who spotted that I had a quick ear which meant I could get through the formal pieces and the training reasonably quickly. She knew I was interested in trying other things too, so she introduced me to the ragtime music of Scott Joplin and some jazz. She also helped me focus on the craft and technicalities of music and to appreciate the composers and musicians of the past. That training proved particularly valuable when I began to write scores.

So by the time I left school I wanted to teach U2 a few things!

I wanted to be in the biggest rock band in the world! But in the meantime I joined a bank with the short-term objective of earning cash to buy more keyboards and become a better attraction for a band. I had also discovered Bruce Springsteen and the punk revolution, new-wave bands like Elvis Costello and the Attractions, and then Duran Duran, Spandau Ballet, Ultravox and electronic music. I wanted to be in a real pox-faced, angst-ridden, cynical, sterile, electronic band.

But the six months I had given myself with the bank actually turned into twelve years. Meantime, I'd moved out of home and was supporting myself. My day job was funding my musical adventures. One of my first bands was Boho, which got a development deal with CBS Records. Such developments gave me the hope that one day I could pack in the job and start recording our album. Boho had good equipment and we spent every spare minute refining our craft. But musicians are often masters of self-delusion, and in time I reached the chilling conclusion that they didn't have the same passion for a career in music I had, so I looked at other options.

I was twenty-eight and this was a hard, cold realisation. I could have stayed in what would inevitably become a cabaret band. There's nothing wrong with that, but it fell far short of my ideals. I wanted a creative career, and never saw a banking career as a serious option. I'd seen too many bitter and resentful guys who'd stayed in the bank and become twisted inside. So leaving the bank wasn't the 'brave' decision I'm often told it was. I didn't want to be forever counting cash into bags and wondering what might have been.

When I hear a piece of my music now I can remember the exact circumstances around the time I composed it, how I was feeling and what was going on in my life. As a composer I more often work to commissions as part of a team, maybe for a film, a show, a television commercial or a documentary that requires a score. I have to develop a creative interpretation of a concept already developed by others. I believe that creativity is 95 per cent perspiration and 5 per cent inspiration. But I never really have a problem coming up with ideas when working with a team. When there's good chemistry it can really get the creative juices going. Of course it doesn't always happen. Sometimes it can be very daunting, painstakingly looking for a thread to help me find the right creative direction. But it's much easier to bring my ideas to a team project where the framework is already narrowed down by specific requirements.

So when it came to composing the music for Michael Flatley's *Lord of the Dance* I knew it had to be fast and frenetic and such that the dancers could dance to it. There's a storyline to the show too, so the dramatic aspects needed to be accentuated. So the blank canvas that a songwriter faces is a much more frightening prospect to me than receiving a script or discussing music ideas with a producer or director. "

FAVOURITE SONG:
One of my favourite songs is 'From Rags to Riches' by the Blue Nile. The album it featured on was my saviour through wet, miserable, cold, winter mornings as I took the bus to the bank wondering if I would ever get that break.

FAVOURITE ALBUM:
A Walk Across the Rooftops by The Blue Nile

BIGGEST INFLUENCE:
Both my parents, particularly my father, have been incredibly supportive. He has a fine strategic business mind and I draw on it to this day. He's a tremendous influence on the way I think, very supportive and never intrusive. He's always been there when I needed him.

63

RONAN KEATING

Born in Dublin in 1977, Ronan Keating first rose to prominence in 1993 as one of the star vocalists with the pop group Boyzone. After four mega-selling albums and countless number one hits all over the world, Keating left the band to pursue a solo career. In 2000 he scored his first solo number one with a cover of the song 'When You Say Nothing At All' written by Don Schlitz and Paul Overstreet. Further accolades came his way with the success of 'Life Is A Rollercoaster' taken from his debut album which was simply called *Ronan*. As well as his musical adventures, Ronan has enjoyed partaking in other challenging projects, including presenting the *Eurovision Song Contest* and guiding Irish supergroup Westlife to chart-topping success as their co-manager. He has also discovered himself as a songwriter, and the success of the song he wrote and recorded with Paul Brady, 'The Long Goodbye', suggests Ronan has several strings to his musical bow.

When I was younger I must have been influenced by what my brothers and sisters were listening to. They had everything from Wham to Sting, from The Police to the Alan Parsons Project. My parents used to listen to Irish country and western, Elvis Presley and Frank Sinatra. So my musical education was just a healthy mix of all that.

The moment when I really noticed that I had a keen interest in music was when my brothers and sisters went to America and I was left in the house on my own. To go from living in such a crazy house with three brothers and a sister, when there was always something going on, to being totally on my own was a strange new experience. I noticed how the house had become very, very quiet and that made me turn to music. I went through all their records and tapes and played them just to entertain myself, I suppose. I just got hooked by it and soon got to the point that I used to run home from school and stay in my bedroom listening to music, day and night.

I joined my first band when I was about thirteen. It was a school band and we did cover versions of songs by Nirvana, Bryan Adams and so on. We even won a few talent shows. I always wanted to have a go at it, always trying to get some-where with my music. So I was in a few bands at school and when I saw the advertisement for what was to become Boyzone I went for it because I thought, "This is what I want on the scale that I want it. I want to make proper records and have a proper career". I also wanted to start writing and do my own thing, and it all fell into place.

I was a late starter going to gigs. I went to gigs where my friends' bands were playing, like the Rock Garden or McGonagles in Dublin, but that was more a social thing. The first proper gig I went to had a huge influence on me. I was about fourteen when I went to see Extreme at the Point Depot in Dublin. They had the huge hit at the time called 'More than

Words'. It was a little bit heavy, but it really impressed me. But my first-ever gig as a performer with Boyzone was an absolute disaster! It was in a place called Toughers in Naas in County Kildare. It was a small gig, with mainly our families making up the audience, as we hadn't got a huge fan base at the time. The single 'Working My Way Back To You' had just come out and was doing well in the Irish charts at the time. But we were so full of shite at the time that we climbed out the back window of the venue after the gig and ran down the road to get into our taxi because we thought we were going to be mobbed! And there was only our family and friends at the gig! That's how feckin' mad we were.

Of course it wasn't inevitable that I would become a singer. I went off to become a garda, did the test and everything, but then Boyzone got in the way! Looking back now, I think I would probably have found some way of having a go at music at some stage. Somehow, or some way, I would have found a way into it.

While I was in Boyzone there was no actual time when I thought I'd had enough of it, but there were plenty of times when I was really down in the dumps. Not just me, but all of us were. There was a trip to Asia; being in Bangkok was such a culture shock at the time for young lads like ourselves. You're a million miles from home where everyone is asleep when you're awake, because of the time zones. Then everyone's awake while you're asleep. That was probably the most difficult period.

I'm not going to say we cried ourselves to sleep. It wasn't that bad, but we were homesick, and lonely, really lonely and all we wanted to do was go home. There were hard times, especially when we travelled long distances from home.

When it comes to influences, my mother was a major influence on me. I believe all mothers are influences on kids in this country, and most lads will tell you that. I don't know what it was, but we were very close, and she is still very important to me. I must also say that Louis Walsh has been a huge influence on me. He has been a great friend, and continues to be a great friend, and he gave me the chance in the beginning. I hope that I've paid him back for everything he has done for us and for me. I have also met many people along the way who have influenced me, everyone from U2 to Brian Kennedy. They have all been fantastic and a great encouragement.

Looking back, I have some great memories in music. The most personal memory for me was having a successful debut solo album. That was a huge deal. Coming away from such a massively successful band as Boyzone, all the pressure was on me to perform. But it worked and that success took a huge weight off my shoulders."

64

RONNIE DREW

Ronnie Drew was born on September 16th, 1934, in Dun Laoghaire, Co Dublin. Equipped with what can be only described as one of the most distinctive voices in Irish music, Ronnie has thrilled audiences worldwide with his work with The Dubliners and as a solo artist. Apart from a break between 1974 and 1978, he played with The Dubliners for an astounding thirty-three years, before going solo in 1995.

" I've never had a 'Saint Paul' experience, so I don't actually have a vivid memory of my first musical experience. Things just seemed to happen. There was no blinding flash. Although the instrument is incidental to what I do, I started off wanting to play guitar. But I gave it up because I'm not a gifted instrumentalist. I play well enough to keep a rhythm going for myself, but I'm more interested in singing and telling stories.

The first man ever to give me a job on the stage was John Molloy at Dublin's Gate Theatre. He heard me one night at a party telling a story and singing an oul' song. I had no aspirations then to go on the stage or anything like that, I just thought it would be nice to do it. So I did, and it just went on from there. I used to feed him with sketches and do sketches with him. I sang when he needed a break and it helped with building my confidence. At first I wasn't nervous apart from the usual fluttering nerves, until one night I got stage fright and it took me twenty years to get over it.

In 1962 I started with The Dubliners in O'Donoghue's pub in Merrion Row. Barney McKenna and myself would go to O'Donoghues so I could get paid because John Molloy lived nearby and we used to meet him there. One night we asked to play in the pub and they agreed, provided we kept the volume down. Subsequently we met Luke Kelly and Ciaran Burke, and that was the real start of The Dubliners. They were great times in lots of ways. You could go into a pub and talk to people, rather than being bombarded with television screens and football like today.

I went to Spain around 1956/57 and was teaching English down there. I didn't have a word of Spanish, but I chanced my arm and managed to learn English better than I knew it before I left. I learned a bit of Spanish as well and I have enough Spanish now that I wouldn't starve if I had to depend on it. When I was a kid I wanted to be a jockey, but I've heard my own grandson saying he wants to be this, that and the other. You hardly pay any attention until they get to a certain age and then you might take them seriously. I never really knew what I wanted to be, and still don't know what I want to be.

People will look at the success of The Dubliners, but success is a very arbitrary word. Because a lot of people perceive you to make a lot of money they call that 'success'. But I've never

ever felt successful. Hundreds of thousands have come to see us over the years, but I have never felt successful. I'm still looking to see what I should be doing and I'm going to keep looking, but at the moment I regard myself as a journeyman. I'll do whatever is going, a bit part in a film, a song, a poem, tell a joke or a story. I enjoy what I do but I am a journeyman, not an artist.

There are certain songs I like singing. I don't write songs but I sing songs hoping to get across what they mean. It's so difficult sometimes, because songwriters spend hours writing songs and then I get up to sing, for example, an anti-war song like 'The Band Played Waltzing Matilda' and they start dancing! They seem incapable of listening to the words. That's an indictment of the punters, not me. But then you get a certain section of the audience, and sometimes entire audiences, who will listen to the song, and that's very gratifying. But the punters are force-fed whatever the market forces tell the radio and television stations to play, because market forces control everything. They direct what's to be played and Rock'n'Roll is now the establishment. Rock'n'Roll is no longer the Rock'n'Roll of the rebel.

One of the most rewarding things I have ever done was the show *Ronnie I Hardly Knew Ya* with Mike Hanrahan at the Andrews Lane Theatre in Dublin. I really enjoyed it because it was my own thing, a bit of me getting across to people, and it's the gig I'm really happiest about over the last forty years. The sponsors were fantastic and the write-ups were nearly off the wall. But I didn't have enough money to publicise it at the time and publicity has become prohibitively expensive through the media. You have to be very wealthy to do it. A certain amount of word of mouth got around, but not enough. Then again, I wouldn't be a fashionable performer either. Certain people are in fashion and people go to see them whether they are good, bad or indifferent. As for boy bands, I don't even think about them. They're just tins of beans being sold for profit. They make lots of money, but sure the gangster Al Capone made a lot of money. If that's all you want and you don't care how you make it, then I'm sure you can make money. I like to do certain things and I need to get paid for doing whatever I'm asked to do, but if I got a million to do something it still wouldn't make me feel any more successful than I feel now."

FAVOURITE SONGS:
I have several favourite songs but no definitive one. One is Joe South's 'Games People Play', or Bessie Smith singing 'Nobody Loves You When You're Down and Out', and some by Frank Sinatra. There are lots of Irish songs I love, but I don't have a favourite. I hear people going to hear a group or a singer who's playing ten gigs and going to all of them. I couldn't be having that. I like to go and see the people and hear the people, but I don't have a fanaticism about any particular music. I like music across the board, including jazz.

65

SAMANTHA MUMBA

Dubliner Samantha Mumba has enjoyed enormous international success since her debut album, *Gotta Tell You*, was released in 2000. A past pupil of the renowned Billy Barry Stage School, Mumba left school aged seventeen to pursue her musical career, and she has since expanded her activities into the area of film. Regarded as one of the most talented pop music exports to emerge from Ireland in the recent past, Samantha looks all set to play a pivotal role in the Irish entertainment business for the foreseeable future.

"I was absolutely obsessed with Michael Jackson when I was a child. His *Thriller* video was like a movie to me. It was around ten minutes long, whereas your average pop music video lasts only as long as the song. When I went to my aunt's house on a Sunday I used to beg her to put that video on. I thought the dancing in it was amazing. This was a real treat for me back then because we didn't have MTV in the house or anything like it. So my aunt's house was my only way of seeing it. I was fascinated by the video, scared of it while at the same time loving every second of it. The tape would be in danger of becoming worn out and eventually my aunt had to hide it from me! So being aware of that music and enjoying it are among my earliest and most vivid memories of music.

As a little girl I never thought of making a career out of music. I suppose I never really thought very seriously when I was growing up as to what I wanted to be. But music had always been the consistent thing in my life right from the early days right up to the present. I've always got a great buzz from it, from the time I started dancing and singing from the age of four onwards. It was a comforting thing, something I could always see myself doing for pleasure. I would fantasise about myself up there singing on stage. But when you are a child you live in fairytale land and you don't really think of the career part of it.

When I think back to the first time I planned to go to a concert it's a sad memory really. I was supposed to go to see Gloria Estefan in Dublin, but unfortunately she was involved in a really bad crash from which she got a really bad back injury and she couldn't do the tour. I loved her, we had bought the tickets and I was so gutted (as any child would be) when I discovered she couldn't make it. But I didn't really go to very many shows as a little girl, though I was appearing more often on stage and on TV from quite young. So in one sense I was going to a lot of music events because I was actually in them, getting a terrific buzz from being up there on the stage, really, really loving it and enjoying the reaction of the audience. Because it was something I was doing from a very early age it didn't feel in any way alien or strange. In fact I always feel most natural when I'm on stage. To be up there performing my own stuff with my own choreography, that is such a huge thing to me. It was always truly exciting and it still is, and I never get blasé about it. Even today my heart is in my mouth every time

I go out on stage.

It wasn't until I reached the age of eleven or twelve that I began to think a little about what I wanted to be when I grew up. I knew I wanted to entertain whether it was singing, dancing or performing. One way or another I knew that I was going to be doing something like that even if I wasn't very specific about it. I believe that even if things hadn't worked out the way they did I would still have been doing it in a different way, maybe working in theatre, or as a dance teacher or just doing small singing gigs.

Apart from my mother there have been many people who have had an influence on my career. Michael Jackson is one, of course, who was a huge, huge, huge influence when I was growing up

Naturally enough there have been moments when I have not enjoyed what I was doing. I remember my first trip to America, when I went for four weeks. It was the longest time I had ever spent away from home in one stretch, and it was also the furthest I had ever been away from familiar surroundings. I wasn't used to the time differences and I ran up huge phone bills in the hotels ringing family and friends back home. Because it was my first trip to the United States we were playing in tiny, tiny venues. I think our first gig was in Texas for a radio station's Hallowe'en Party, and I remember thinking "Oh my God, this is awful!" We were staying in dreadful hotels and myself and the dancers, the whole bunch of us, we were all just so depressed. It was right before Christmas and I thought I was going to crack up, but I managed to get home the day before Christmas Eve. Getting home saved me. But the trip certainly paid off in terms of building up my name in the USA.

The best moment of my career would have to be my first day on the movie set of *Time Machine*, arriving at Warner Brothers studio, the feeling of being in Hollywood and going to my very own trailer. I just went "Wow, this is crazee!" It was so exciting. The huge movie sets were just breathtaking to look at, not to mention the trailers and the crew. It was all just so Hollywood, and so very glamorous, although many of the jobs in the movie business aren't glamorous at all. In fact, the single thing that turned out to be so different from how anyone might imagine it to be was discovering how many movie industry jobs are just normal and very boring behind the scenes. But overall it was a truly fantastic experience.

Even as recently as four years ago I would not have thought that performing and acting would have become my life. Nor could I have foreseen all the exciting things that have happened to me, the places I've been and the people I've met and worked with, including UNICEF. So the last couple of years have been truly fantastic. Hopefully my future recordings will do well too, and I'm hoping to continue working on new movie projects. But I never think too far ahead in case I jinx myself!"

FAVOURITE SINGER: Michael Jackson

FAVOURITE SONG: *Thriller* by Michael Jackson

FAVOURITE ALBUM: India Arie *Acoustic Soul*

66

SEAN KEANE

Born into the famously musical Keane family in Caherlistrane in Co. Galway, singer Sean Keane has been described by the London *Independent* as 'the greatest Irish musical find of the nineties'. Having recorded five solo albums since 1994, he has established himself as one of Ireland's most esteemed and talented singers. Brother of the equally renowned Dolores Keane, he has won more than thirteen All-Ireland titles for his unique singing style and has collaborated with outstanding singers and musicians, including the 'fifth Beatle', Sir George Martin.

When I consider what influenced me as a singer I go back to one of my first musical memories. I was around at my grandmother's house when I was about three or four years of age. A blind neighbour called Ulick McDara came into the house and sang songs to us. He was dictating a song called 'Erin's Lovely Home' to my grandmother when a row broke out between her and himself as to whether the words of the melody were fitting together. They both seemed ancient to me at the time, in their late seventies or eighties.

The result of the argument was that my grandmother made a ball of the piece of paper on which she was writing the words and threw it on to the fire, where it promptly disappeared in a blaze. That was the end of the argument, but for a long time afterwards I very vividly remembered the line of the song that they were arguing so much about that day, such is the impression that incident made on me. That line went "There are seven links upon my chain and every link a year. It's then I can return again to the arms of my dear". But the matter didn't end with the ball of paper in the fire. When I went to Inishbofin about fifteen or sixteen years ago I chanced to meet a man living there called Michael Joe Hallam who had the same song that they were arguing about that day. But Michael Joe had it with a different melody to Ulick MacDara. So from Michael Joe I got the remainder of the words that had been lost that day because of the argument and I recorded the song on my first album!

The first concert I remember going to was a Liam Clancy and Tommy Makem concert at the Odeon Cinema in Tuam in Co Galway. I would have been about six or seven and they were so good they blew me away. They had a huge effect on me, they were so gifted together, a real 'Hot Act', great musically, but equally great as entertainers and communicators. They had a wonderful way with an audience and there was so much fun going on it felt to me that they hardly played any songs at all! There was so much banter coming out of them that you didn't notice the two hours going by. In fact it felt more like five minutes. To me that was a key part of the magic of music, the way you'd get lost in that mysterious world with the musicians and the audience. But I could be equally impressed at home sitting by the fireplace listening to Joe Holmes and the rest of the family singing a song and playing a tune.

But music hasn't always been my profession. I started off welding and engineering with Steel Fabrication before I became a professional musician. My father and brother had a workshop at home and I had been welding since I was about ten or so, taking on odd jobs for farmers who needed to have their machinery fixed and so on. I also enjoyed mixing the two, the welding and the music.

I was working away by day and singing at night, going away at weekends to sing at festivals and wherever else I could, and the music just took up more and more of my time. Something had to go and I had to make a decision, whether I was going to stay working or move more towards the music. So I went with the music to try it for a while and I'm still at it and I'm still very happy.

I'm not really aware of who actually influences me, although the initial interest in music came maybe more from my mother's side of the family. Her brothers and her relatives all sang and played various instruments, but so did my father's side of the family. I've kind of developed a way of doing things my own way musically. Others say that I sort of make a song my own. When I hear a song that I want to sing I will sing it the way I feel it, regardless of what genre it comes from. If it can move me then I would hope to move other people when I sing it. Basically I have to be true to the song and the lyric and it has to be true to me. I'm wide open to good music and there are only two categories of music to me, good and bad. I prefer to hear as much good music as I can of any kind - rock, folk, trad, jazz or classical. It doesn't matter which genre; it's either good or bad.

I was lucky enough to be born with the gift of a good voice, but just because I was born into a family steeped in the deep tradition of Irish music doesn't mean I should have to stick to that one style. If I just sang traditional songs I would be denying the talent I was given and also denying the pleasure of singing all the great music and songs that are out there in all kinds of music styles. Fabulous music is being written here and all over the world, and I would hate to say that I cannot sing this or that song just because I'm a traditional singer. That, to me, would be totally wrong."

67

SIX

Six were formed from over five thousand auditionees who took part in the RTE TV programme, *Popstars*. From this 13-part series six individual performers were chosen: Andrew Orr, Liam McKenna, Sarah Keating, Emma O'Driscoll, Sinead Shepard and Kyle Anderson. Their debut single 'There's A Whole lot of Loving Going On' was recorded with the legendary producer Pete Waterman in London. Released in February 2002, in its first week it debuted at Number 1 in the Irish charts and became the fastest-ever-selling single in Ireland. It also achieved the biggest first-week sales by any non-charity record, became the biggest selling single of 2002 and actually sold more in its first week than the rest of Top 10 put together! The single remained at Number 1 here for four weeks and sold more than 120,000 copies.

ANDREW ORR

"I started singing when I was about ten. I was in the school choir and I later became a busker on Grafton Street in Dublin. Then I played in different bands in pubs, mainly rock music, as indie rock was what I grew up listening to.

My mum and dad didn't really have an influence on me musically. My dad wouldn't be into music at all, and my mother would listen to bands like the Beach Boys, although she was never a big music fan. It was my friends and the people who I grew up with at school who got me into music.

My biggest influence has to be Bono from U2. The guy is an absolute legend and he has proven that even if you come from a small island like Ireland there is nothing to stop you from taking your music all over the world. The guy is living proof that dreams can come true. One of the songs that I sang when I was auditioning for Six was 'With or Without You' by U2. I think they are an amazing group and I used to sing a lot of their songs in my busking days."

FAVOURITE ALBUM: REM's *Automatic for the People*

FAVOURITE SONG: Metallica's 'Unforgiven' and Huey Lewis and the News' ''The Power of Love'.

EMMA O'DRISCOLL

"I've been singing and dancing since I was teeny, doing Irish dancing and jigging around the house. I used to go into my next-door neighbour so he would tape me singing for his tape recorder when I was about five or so. When I was about seven I joined a choir with my two older sisters. I always wanted to be on the stage, always wanted to dance around the sitting room, singing in front of everybody. That's just the way I grew up, really.

One of my biggest influences when I was small was Kylie Minogue. I got her single, 'I Should Be So Lucky', for my seventh birthday. I was just awestruck walking around with this record in my hand. At the time I really didn't say it to anybody, but I wanted to be Kylie. My mom used to play her old sixties vinyl records and I would dance around and hide behind the curtains and act out the songs. I started joining traditional groups when I got a bit bigger. I got more of a taste for it and started performing on stage.

As I became older, about fourteen or fifteen, my aunt would bring me into a pub, with my mum and dad, and they would say, ''You're not allowed to drink, but go up on the stage and sing''. My aunt would sing on stage and she would encourage me up for a song or two songs. Then she would make me go home and learn a new song for the rest of the week. My life seemed to revolve around music even though at the time I didn't realise I wanted a career out of it. I just saw it as a hobby, but I was totally obsessed with it.

As I got older I realised that this is what I wanted to do. It really sank in when I was fifteen and I went off and made a demo CD and I didn't want to stop after that. I wasn't going to give in until I made it.''

FAVOURITE ALBUM: All of Whitney Houston's albums. Her voice is excellent. Nobody can deny that.

FAVOURITE SONG: The first singing contest I won was with Whitney Houston's 'Greatest Love'. It was my dad's suggestion. I also sang it at the auditions for *Popstars,* so maybe that song is my favourite because it has a lot of meaning for me now and I've always had good luck with it.

BIGGEST INFLUENCES: Whitney Houston, Celine Dion, Kylie Minogue and Anastasia.

LIAM McKENNA
  ❝ In the days when Michael Jackson was really big I used to be a big, big Michael Jackson fan. I remember the *Thriller* and *Bad* videos, the moon walking, the glove, all of that and I remember thinking, ''Wow, wouldn't it be brilliant to be able to do that.''

I always wanted to be a singer, but I was realistic enough to accept that I probably wasn't going to get a chance to do it. I was of the impression that I'd have to go and train to do whatever job I could, and maybe work with computers or whatever, but music was always in the back of my mind. I think I would never have been very happy if I hadn't got the chance to go for it. That's why I kept trying and trying.

I have so many good memories that it's hard to pick one. As a band we have done things that not one of us could have dreamt of. You dream of one day becoming a successful singer and when you achieve that there is so much that it brings to you. But perhaps my favourite memory is of the day I got into the band, because that's what started it all off for us. My biggest influence is Westlife because we are such good friends with the members of the band. We look up to them and aspire to be like them. To be even half as successful, that would be enough for us.''

SARAH KEATING
  ❝ Music has always been in the house for as far back as I can remember. My dad is a singer and musician, and since I was knee high he encouraged every member of the family

to sing. On my mother's side of the family there are several good songwriters. My uncle used to play for The Saw Doctors and co-wrote some of their songs, so he would have been a big influence on my life when I was growing up.

Music-wise, the first show I ever performed in was when I was six, singing 'Puff The Magic Dragon'. That was my first-ever experience of performing music to an audience. I'm sure there is a video copy of it out there somewhere, but I don't have one, thank God! Since then I've been in shows, musicals and pantos, and I've always been encouraged by my family. It's all I ever wanted to do.

My mother is a teacher, so she regularly said to me, "If you didn't want to go singing professionally then you could be a teacher". When I was thirteen or fourteen I was in a performing arts school in Galway and I wanted to continue doing it professionally. I intended going over to England to audition for a stage school there, but, as it turned out, my parents felt that I was too young to go on my own. It's probably just as well, seeing how things worked out so much for the better! But from that age I always had it as a dream, and I could never seriously picture myself doing anything other than singing."

FAVOURITE SONG:
'Bridge Over Troubled Water' by Simon and Garfunkel.

BIGGEST INFLUENCE:
My Uncle Pauric who encouraged me throughout the years.

FAVOURITE ALBUM:
Dido's *No Angel*

SINEAD SHEPARD

"The film *Dirty Dancing* brings back early memories for me. I remember seeing all the great dancing and singing in it. My dad bought me the soundtrack album and I used to sing all the songs and dance around the living room to it. Then it was Kylie Minogue, and after seeing her do 'The Locomotion' I decided that I wanted be famous.

When I was seven my parents and grandparents were in a musical in our home-town in Cork and they formed a community theatre there. So one night when they couldn't get a babysitter they brought me along with them. So I went straight up to the director and asked if I could have a small part in the play and he said "Yes!" From then on I would do all the shows at home and go for every audition that was ever held. So it all started from when I was a baba!

During secondary school I was studying for the Leaving Cert and I came out of school one day and I said to my granddad in the car going home, "I love school and I don't mind studying, but I never feel fulfilled when I come out of there". But his response was like "What are you on about? Put the head down in the books and stop daydreaming". But I believed I was meant for something else. I wanted to be in the spotlight.

My parents were very encouraging. They pushed me all the time and would tell me to go for all the auditions, which I did. Every time you are turned down, you promise yourself you're never going for another one. But then another one comes up and you try again. So even if I wasn't doing what I do now with this band I'd be auditioning today somewhere else, looking for that big break."

FAVOURITE ALBUM:
Alicia Keys *Songs in A Minor*

BIGGEST INFLUENCE:
Bands like Boyzone and Westlife who have made it
worldwide.

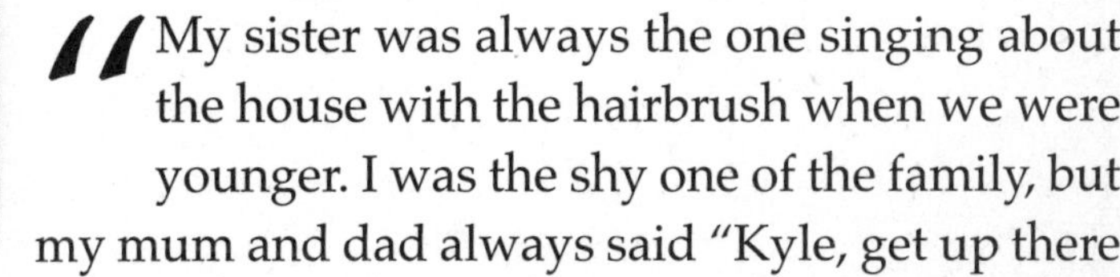

KYLE ANDERSON

"My sister was always the one singing about the house with the hairbrush when we were younger. I was the shy one of the family, but my mum and dad always said "Kyle, get up there and sing away and see what you can do". I went to singing lessons back then and won a few competitions in the Northern Ireland region. From there I just continued on singing until I stopped and played a bit of rugby instead. I didn't really go back into singing until I went to the *Popstars* auditions.

My first two loves are music and rugby, but I always said that rugby would win. My dad played for Ulster and I basically wanted to follow in his footsteps. But I got injured, started singing and then got into the band. I sometimes ask myself "What if?", because the morning of the audition for *Popstars* I was meant to play a rugby match but it was cancelled due to bad weather, so it's just by chance that I went up to the audition. It's strange the way it happened but I'm glad that it did."

FAVOURITE SONG:
'Thriller' by Michael Jackson

BIGGEST INFLUENCE:
Westlife - the first time I ever had the urge to be in a band
was after seeing them in the Odyssey in Belfast.

FAVOURITE ALBUM:
U2's *The Joshua Tree* and all the albums by The Beatles.

68

SONNY CONDELL

As a solo songwriter-performer and the driving force behind two Irish groups, Scullion and Tír Na nÓg, Sonny Condell occupies an almost unrivalled place in the Irish musical landscape. From inauspicious beginnings improvising on old barrels and singing with his relatives in a County Wicklow farm shed, he's been a consistent presence on the Irish music scene for over thirty years. From the late sixties onwards, Sonny travelled throughout the UK as one half of the folk-rock duo, Tír Na nÓg, sharing stages with acts of the calibre of Cat Stevens, Procol Harum and Supertramp. In 1979 he helped form the band Scullion with Philip King, subsequently releasing three albums regarded by many as among the finest this country has produced. Thirty years after he began the journey that saw him influence generations of Irish singers and songwriters, Sonny Condell remains a formidable musical force and one of Ireland's most respected writers and performers.

"My father has probably been one of the key factors that led to my becoming a musician. He loved music and was an enthusiastic record collector. Back in the 1950's he always had a gramophone player of some kind at home and he would play it at night after a hard day's work at the farm. He would listen to classical music mostly, but he became interested in Portuguese music and all sorts of things which were inspiring to listen to. He always tried to have a good quality gramophone player, and as time went on he went in for the serious hi-fi stuff. I might be going to bed while listening to some operatic singing he'd have on. There was real depth in that music which made a huge difference to the way I learned to listen to music.

I started playing instruments when I went to boarding schools. Some of the lads played guitars and other stuff and I just tried to keep up with them. I remember starting off playing the drums, or trying to! But I never really had a full kit, and that didn't help.

Then I was given a present of a guitar by a friend at home in Wicklow and that really helped. I took the guitar to school and eventually got better at keeping up with the other lads. Usually I was a chord or two behind them, but gradually I became very interested in the possibilities of the instrument. The lads would have played Dylan songs and pop songs of the time, and that's how I learned how to play guitar, by trying to keep up with them.

The first gigs I ever went to were the various school dances that I attended as a schoolboy. I remember seeing a Dublin band called The Creatures in a place called the Caroline Club which was in Dun Laoghaire. They were one of the few Irish 'beat groups', as we called them, to get a record contract, and I was really knocked out by them. I thought they were fantastic as a live act. But in general I've never been one for going to gigs, preferring playing to listening, doing gigs rather than going to gigs.

When I was younger I honestly didn't know what I wanted to be in terms of earning a living. The obvious thing would have been to go into farming, something to do with the land. But I'd had enough of that by the time I reached eighteen or so. I wasn't brilliant academically at school. Towards the end of my schooldays I found myself increasingly concentrating on music and writing more of my own material. I began to feel that it might have possibilities as a way of life, even if there wasn't a living to be made out of it. So I began to move in that direction. Even after school I worked in some shops in Dublin. But I hated it and music became the only thing that I could at least be good at and enjoy.

The obvious early influences on me were people like the Beach Boys, The Beatles, Nick Drake. There wasn't any one thing that put the cap on it, more a combination of all these artists who were each very inspiring in different ways at certain moments. I remember having a bath at school and The Beatles came on the radio and the hairs on the back of my neck just stood up. It was their first single 'Love Me Do', and to me it was electrifying. It cut like a knife through the type of music that was around at the time.

Moving to London in May of 1970 was a real eye-opener and it had a huge bearing on the development of my career. Leo O'Kelly and I travelled all over playing in folk clubs. I remember Don Partridge had a hit at that time. And I remember even before we left Ireland, Leo would listen to lots of different types of music, and he introduced me to songs by Joni Mitchell and Donovan.

I believe that inspiration must keep on coming and each generation has a number of people who could be regarded as supreme sources of inspiration. But maybe there's so much music around now, and so many kinds of music, that it is harder to pinpoint anything specific in the whole spectrum that I could say truly inspires me. When a new record came out back in my early years it was played all the time on the radio, so maybe it was easier to focus in on it and really get into it and know every detail of it.

Personally, I'm always looking forward rather than looking back. I'd like to think music will bring me the same pure joy in the future as it did in the past."

69

THE DEVLINS

Colin Devlin,
guitarist, vocalist

Formed in Dublin in the early 1990s by brothers Colin (vocals/guitar) and Peter Devlin (bass/vocals), the alternative rock group, The Devlins, gained international acclaim with the release of their 1994 major-label debut, *Drift*. Three years later the group returned with 1997's Waiting, released on the Radio Universe label. More recently The Devlins have enjoyed even further success with their third album, *Consent*, and they continue to give sell-out concerts in Ireland and all across Europe.

❝ My parents are not musicians, but they love music every bit as much as I do. My most vivid memory of music goes back to when I was driving in their car subliminally memorising what The Beatles played on an 8-track stereo. I was always listening to music, not necessarily on the radio, but the Walkman had just been invented when I was a teenager, and most of my time was spent listening to music that way.

I remember very well the first concert I ever went to. I was very young and it was a Boney M concert. I remember being very close to the stage and being able to see everything. I was probably six or seven at the time. My brother Peter brought me to my first 'proper' gig when I was about fourteen. We went to see *Everything but the Girl* at the TV Club in Dublin which is now sadly demolished. It was so exciting, and made all the better by the fact that I had my first underage pint that same night.

My first proper gig as a performer was for a school talent contest, which luckily we won. But as I grew older I had no idea what I wanted to do when I grew up. So it came as a great relief when I discovered I had a talent for music. This came quite late, actually, when I was about sixteen. Looking back I can see that I've only been allowed to become who I am through the encouragement of my family and friends. Peter, who is the other half of The Devlins, was always a great inspiration and encouragement to me, and he still is today.

I've had some great memories during my time in the music business. The best was probably playing at Red Rocks in Colorado. Hearing your voice reverberating around a canyon at sunset, with 20,000 people listening, that's a truly beautiful experience. Also when you finish an album, and listen back to what you've just created, that gives you a wonderful feeling.

Of course there have been times when, because of all the work involved in keeping the show on the road, you can feel frustrated and I'm sure the time will eventually come when I'll feel I've had enough of the music business. But until then I'll keep giving it all I've got and enjoy it as much as I can."

FAVOURITE SONG:

My favourite song is probably 'Orpheus' by David Sylvain. It's from an album called *Secrets of the Beehive*. That record has a wonderful timeless mood, which is something as The Devlins we try to achieve on all our records.

FAVOURITE ARTISTS:

Among my favourite artists are The Blue Nile, Leonard Cohen, U2, David Bowie, Tori Amos, The Stones, and Bob Dylan . . . all true survivors.

70

THE REVS

Rory Gallagher, vocals, bass guitar

The Revs are a three-piece rock band from Donegal comprising Rory Gallagher (bass guitar/vocals), John McIntyre (guitar/vocals) and Micky O'Donnell (drums). Described by several music industry insiders as the Irish success story of 2002, The Revs picked up three music industry awards and a gold album, as well as scoring a major European distribution deal with Sony. Their sound has been described as an amalgam of The Police, Supergrass, The Who, and Semisonic on speed, with a live energy reminiscent of Green Day, Smashing Pumpkins and the Violent Femmes. In live performance they demonstrate musical skills way beyond their tender years.

" My most vivid early memory of music is playing drums to Joan Armatrading's 'Me Myself I' in the sitting room of our old house in Parkhead in Killybegs. My parents bought me a 'top of the pops' drum kit when I was three and I could keep the beat with the records by the time I was four. My parents' record collection included a lot of albums by Steely Dan and The Police, so that didn't make learning very easy for me! But it's mad really, because I was drumming along with 'Roxanne' by The Police when I was four! It has fairly complex drumming by Stewart Copeland, so I think if anyone wants their child to become a musician they should skip Barney and S Club 7 and play them Mozart or any of the greats and it will benefit the child so much more.

My parents played in a pop covers band called Pluto, so the radio was constantly on in our house. I think my brain has been forever contaminated with some really dodgy eighties melodies. When I became interested in music my favourite DJ was Dave Fanning on 2FM. I used to do my homework with the radio turned to his show every night from the age of twelve onwards. I still remember the Fleetwood Mac riff he used to open the show with. I used to open my schoolbag at the very same time.

I like to claim that as my parents were in a band I was still in the womb when I went to my first gig. But I got up on stage and drummed with them when I was four.

The first big gig I went to was the Red Hot Chili Peppers at The Point in 1994. Ireland had not yet been hit by the economic boom of a few years later, so it was a big deal to see a band back then. We would wait for months, queuing for tickets outside the Melody Maker shop in Donegal town. Now there's a big US band playing in Dublin nearly every week, so it's like . . . "Oh, who is it this week? The Foo Fighters? Yeah, sure. What's 60 euros?" But that earlier buzz is gone a bit. I might be wrong, but the fans probably don't get as excited as I did when I was fourteen.

The first serious gig I ever played at was in the secondary school gym with my first band, Aftermath. We practised the same five songs for a month! I can still remember them -

'Smells Like Teen Spirit' by Nirvana, 'Smoke On the Water' by Deep Purple, 'Enter Sandman' by Metallica, 'All Right Now' by Free (oh God!) and 'Fear Of The Dark' by Iron Maiden. The only note our bass guitar player, Phelim, knew was G, which made things a tad difficult.

For a while I wanted to be an English teacher as I always loved writing and reading, but I changed my mind when I only got 355 points in the Leaving Cert! Damn you, musical distraction, damn you!

It's hard to pick my best moment in music. There are so many different things to excite you in music, like when you hear the final mix of a song you wrote and it sounds exactly like you intended. Or when you don't have to sing the chorus because the crowd are singing it. Or when you hear your single has gone into the charts and you come back from a gig to turn on Aertel and there you are, crammed in between Coldplay and J- Lo. Or when Larry Mullen and the Lads say, "Well done, you deserve it", or when you walk out onto the same stage you watched Green Day and The Prodigy play the day before and 40,000 people go, "Yeay!!"

Then again, it could be shaking hands with Shay Given and Damien Duff while you're on your way to the stage to play in front of thousands of Irish fans. Or when you hit the first chord of a song and you catch Slane Castle in the corner of your eye. Or when you realise you're gonna be able to spend some time in the studio and come out with something that Sony are gonna release in other countries. The truth is, it's all great!

When the Revs got together in 2000 we played four nights a week for £30 each a night, but we didn't give a shite. We were having a ball, and it showed in our stage presence and in the music. Most people who get frustrated with the music business are usually only in it for the fame or the money. It helps when you just enjoy the music."

FAVOURITE SONGS:

It's impossible to have a favourite song or artist, as music reflects the soul and there are thousands of different emotions you can feel in a day. So one song isn't gonna keep you interested for too long. But I'll name some that have meant a lot to me: The Beatles' 'A Day In The Life', 'Blackbird', 'In My Life', 'Norwegian Wood', Strawberry Fields Forever'; John Lennon's 'Instant Karma' and 'Oh My Love'; The Police's 'Wrapped Around Your Finger' and 'Bring On The Night'; U2's '11 O'clock Tick Tock', 'With Or Without You' and 'Stay'; Sarah McLachlan's 'Angel'; The Pogues' 'Fairytale Of New York' and 'Fiesta'; The Waterboys' 'Fisherman's Blues'; Nirvana's 'All Apologies', 'Heart-shaped Box'; Radiohead's 'Pyramid Song' and 'Subterranean Homesick Alien'; Bonnie Raitt's 'I Can't Make You Love Me' . . . I'd better stop or I'll fill the book!

PS - I also love Mozart's *Jupiter Symphony* and his *Requiem*.

71

THE
SAW DOCTORS Leo Moran, guitarist

Born in Tuam, Co Galway, guitarist Leo Moran was one of the founding members of the legendary Saw Doctors. With the success of singles, 'N17' and 'I Useta Love Her', to their credit, The Saw Doctors have enjoyed tremendous success across Europe and even more so in the US. Indeed, 'I Useta Love Her' become one of the biggest selling singles in the history of the Irish charts. Adding traditional and folk flavours to a solid pop-rock base, The Saw Doctors have released six albums to date. Their compilation "Best Of" album, *Play It Again Sham*, was released to considerable acclaim in 2003.

"I have a lot of memories of music, back to hearing my grandfather singing 'The West's Awake' at a 'do' in our house one time when I was very young. My father is one of those people who's a drummer but doesn't know it. He goes around playing rhythms on tables and any other surface he can find. Despite that, there wasn't much music played in his family. But my mother's family was different. Her brother is a great singer and musician and her father was a lovely singer and a brilliant musician too as well as being a big John McCormack fan. I also remember Abba coming on the scene for the first time when I was in sixth class and I bought their *Greatest Hits* album.

Those were inspirational memories with feelings of admiration, because you saw and heard people doing things and you realised that you would love to have a go at doing stuff like that too. Thinking back to Abba, I imagine it was the hormones. I was about eleven or twelve and I was beginning to realise that there was an awful lot of fun to be had out there!

Very shortly after that, the punk thing kicked in. Punk was right up our street and came at just the right time in our lives. It was fantastic. There was a whole gang of us in Tuam in County Galway who took to the punk thing immediately. It was so much fun. From the music point of view, anybody could have a go at it. With punk you didn't have to be a virtuoso musician and you didn't have to go to music college before you could join a band. Better still, you could call your band any name you wanted. You could use any words you wanted in your songs. Discovering all that is magic when you're young, and punk brought us a great sense of independence, fun and rebelliousness.

So right up until I was fifteen I wanted to be a member of a band. Then the urge went away for a long time. There was a band in Tuam called Blaze X that my friend Davy Carton was in. They were fantastic. They were as good as the records we were buying at that time, and I was probably their biggest fan. They didn't last very long, unfortunately, but they had that special X factor that just takes bands above the ordinary. They were total magic.

After they broke up in 1981 we didn't play or listen to a whole lot of music for a while. Davy was living up near Clarewater at the time and those songs from Blaze X were still hanging around, songs that I knew I loved and that I thought other people might love if they got to hear them. So from there on, myself and Davy started to get together to sing a few of the songs and in that way it all started. It wasn't that either of us at the time wanted to be a pop star, and it became more of a hobby. We simply liked doing the songs. That was a much more relaxed way of starting a band. We weren't looking at it as a career thing as at that stage I had no huge aspirations. The band just fell together in and around the songs.

By the time The Saw Doctors had really kicked into gear around 1987 I was in my early to mid-twenties and was therefore much more relaxed about the whole thing. We weren't trying too hard, to be honest. That's not to say we didn't put a lot of effort into it, but we had got all that silly ambitious thought process out of our heads by that stage.

But at times your brain might be almost overcome with trying to think of things to do with the band. Projects need that kind of process to get them off the ground. You need people to be thinking all the time, looking for new ways of doing things and so on, but we didn't have the aspirations of being pop stars, although we were accidentally nearly cast into that role for a while.

I love all aspects of music. I love being part of a team and I love seeing the fruits of teamwork becoming bigger than the individual parts. I love the songs, I love the gigs, I love recording, I love the travelling and I have never felt frustrated enough to pack it all in. Others are probably different, but I've never thought I don't want to do this any more, or that there was something else that I would prefer to do. That thought has never struck since I started off with The Saw Doctors. It will take something very entertaining, satisfying and enjoyable in order to shift my interests away from music. I can't even imagine what it would be.

I have had many influences and inspirations. A huge inspiration deep down was my grandfather, even though it mightn't have been apparent on the surface. Pauric Stephens, who writes songs with us, was a huge inspiration to me too. He demonstrated to us as a band the fun you could have expressing aspects of your locality and the idiosyncrasies of the local language in the songs. As soon as we found that key, and we realised we'd found the key. It was like finding the door to the new level of fun we could have just by being ourselves. From then on, the songs almost made themselves up.

I love Bruce Springsteen, and the likes of Tom Waits and the Sex Pistols. They were doing what we were doing, expressing themselves on their own terms, in their own universe. When we found that we could do that too, coming from where we were coming, it all just fell into place.

I don't look to the future. I was never a fan of the song 'One Day at a Time' by Gloria, but it's hard to argue with the sentiment of those lyrics. You can't really plan too far ahead. There are so many obstacles that you can come up against if you start planning things too rigidly. All the great things that have happened to the band along the way came out of the blue at short notice, and that suits me fine."

FAVOURITE ALBUM:
Darkness On The Edge Of Town, *Tunnel Of Love* or *Nebraska*, all by Bruce Springsteen.

FAVOURITE SONG:
I can't really say, because there are too many.

72

SOMETHING HAPPENS

Tom Dunne, lead singer / songwriter

Born in Dublin, Tom Dunne first shot to the attention of Irish rock and pop audiences as lead singer and main songwriter with the band, Something Happens. The band made several classy albums for Virgin Records, scored numerous hit singles, toured the world and generally enjoyed themselves as much as their audiences. Their single, 'Parachute', was voted the best-ever single by an Irish act by *Hot Press* readers and 2FM listeners. More recently, Dunne has enjoyed a successful broadcasting career as a music presenter on RTE television and on Today FM's *Pet Sounds,* winning him a coveted *Hot Press* National TV and Radio Award in 1999. He was also voted best Radio DJ at the 2002 Meteor Irish Music Awards.

" My earliest childhood memory of music could also have been my last musical memory! When I was ill with a fever as a child my folks made a bed for me downstairs, and all I could hear for days on end was 'Michelle' by The Beatles. I remember the excitement of getting somebody to turn it up every time it came on. Being as melodramatic then as I am now, I thought I was at death's door, and can remember thinking, "Well, at least the music was lovely!"

Radio had a huge influence on me. I was a bit studious and possibly a little withdrawn, so I didn't mind a long night with the schoolbooks as long as I had a radio. I remember when Dave Fanning came on at midnight on 2FM I would often listen to the end of his show, loving every note.

Songs have always had the ability to stop me in my tracks in a way that's sometimes hard to explain. I still remember hearing the Californian singer-songwriter Stephen Bishop singing 'Little Italy' for the first time and having to put down my pen to stare at the radio. Stephen would later be revealed to me as a man in a dodgy white suit with the type of facial hair suggestive of a male-bonding movie like *Philadelphia*. However, when Chaka Khan starts to sing whatever she sings (something about Rosie being old enough to live her own life), even the birds in the trees pay attention.

When Punk arrived, radio took on a wartime quality. To hear The Clash or The Jam or Elvis Costello was like receiving news from the front, and the inclusion of Irish bands was incredibly exciting. When bands from my generation started to make their presence felt, it was like a drug, and you were inspired to do the same. You were convinced that most commercial music was crap and that it was our responsibility to show them the error of their ways. So hearing U2 on Larry Gogan's Top 40 was like an away win in Europe - dramatic, heroic, brilliant.

My parents didn't have a musical background, but they both loved music and both sang. My mother sang in the house all the time, night or day, even at the kitchen sink as she did the washing, and my dad sang at parties. Given the right circumstances, my dad was a bit of an entertainer and was funny with it. My mother needs more coaxing, although she has a beautiful voice. I stayed with her last Christmas Eve, and as I lay in bed at about 2 a.m. she started singing gently. There wasn't a sound in the house, just me in my dad's old room and the gentle, almost other-worldly voice of my mother (who's now eighty) singing a song from a generation now mostly gone. It was gorgeous and very moving. She's a real treasure.

The first gig I went to was in 1977. Fuelled by our adventures in the Gaeltacht, my friend Cormac and I worked up the courage to go 'into town' to a gig. We had to pretend to be over eighteen, but the band we got to see was Midnight Well with Thom Moore and Janie Cribbs. We loved the gig, and their eponymous album is still worth searching out.

The first gig I played was in 1981 with my first-ever band, The End. We supported The New Versions in McGonagles in Dublin. Prior to the gig we had rehearsed in Cormac's dad's barber shop. I had only ever sung into a hairbrush, so when the mike didn't work I didn't notice. After two songs a girl pulled my shoe and said "Your mike's not switched on!" I duly discovered the on/off switch and switched it on to a great round of applause!

When I was younger, the idea of being a professional musician was fanciful. As a kid I dreamt of being an archaeologist, but later I started leaning towards the sciences because I thought maths was very easy. By the time I was studying for my Leaving Cert I wanted either to be a writer, probably a journalist, or an engineer. Ironically I opted for engineering on the advice of a journalist. But although I loved UCD my heart was always in music. In retrospect it seems I lacked the courage to have gone for it earlier.

There have been so many good memories. The first time we sold out the National Stadium in Dublin was very special. We went from doing The Underground, a small venue in Dame Street, to the Stadium in the course of only about eighteen months. So imagine the feeling on stage when we surveyed 2,500 people who'd all come to see us. I think bands can be like people; they have an infancy and a period of blissful youthful innocence, of energy and enthusiasm, followed by life experiences that make them mature and sometimes more inhibited and less able to just let go. That first Stadium show was blissful youth, pure magic.

Of course the business can be frustrating at times, and not just because of all the necessary hard work. For a band to fire on all cylinders you have to get so many things right, the band itself, to management, record company, producers, photographers, sleeve designers, booking agents. The list is almost endless.

It seems when it works they all just fall into step together, but when it goes wrong they are all completely out of kilter and you don't know where to start to try putting it right. And then it comes down to you to perform, perhaps to sing in a venue you're not suited to, to an audience with different tastes, at the wrong time for the wrong reasons. If it doesn't get fixed, you eventually just stop."

FAVOURITE SONG:
It's hard to pick just one. I tend to nominate 'God Only Knows' by the Beach Boys because it's so perfect. It epitomises the charm of pop music, its optimism in the face of all reality. It's like a prayer.

FAVOURITE ALBUM:
I'd select *Pet Sounds* by the Beach Boys for the same reason, the breadth of its ambition. But I might also mention *Nevermind* by Nirvana and *Doolittle* by The Pixies, two albums that stopped me in my tracks.

73

TOMMY FLEMING

Sligo-born Tommy Fleming has had a remarkable career, from singing with the Phil Coulter Orchestra to touring with legendary traditional act De Danann and his four top selling albums as a solo artist. His interpretations of classic songs such as 'Danny Boy' and 'Hard Times', not to mention his unique delivery of songs written for him by Irish songwriters Jimmy MacCarthy and Christie Hennessy, have brought him countless plaudits. Such is Tommy's personal resilience that he overcame a career-threatening injury after a car crash in 1998 and continues to record and entertain audiences across Ireland, the USA, Australia and Europe. His *Contender* album introduced him to audiences as far away as Japan, but one of his biggest personal achievements was working in general healthcare nutrition in South Sudan on behalf of GOAL.

" There's music on both sides of my family going back through the generations. Grandparents, grand-uncles and grand-aunts provided music, song and dance for the local house dances in their day. That musical tradition has carried down to the current generation. We didn't play any instruments in our family, but all of us could sing and dance. When relatives returned from England for holidays, music, singing and dancing were very much to the fore.

So there was always music at home when I was young. The radio was on all day, and we had an old red record-player a cousin of my dad's gave us for Christmas. He'd send us all sorts of records, and we'd be so excited getting in from school to discover he'd sent another batch. We didn't mind what they were. They ranged from céili bands like the Tulla and Gallowglass to collections of Jim Reeves and Val Doonican. My mother is still a big Jim Reeves fan, so we listened to him over and over. When Jim was given a rest, we often turned to a collection of Sixties No. 1s. We still occasionally take them out to play, and although they're slightly scratched, the songs sound as good as ever.

I'm the youngest of six, and as my older brothers and sisters started to buy records I was introduced to a much wider range of music. I remember the John Travolta craze of *Saturday Night Fever* and *Grease*. My sisters had them all. One of my brothers was a mad Status Quo fan (still is), so from *Ma Kelly's Greasy Spoon* to *Rockin' All Over The World* we had all their albums too. One of my early favourites from when I was about seven was Boney M, and the first single I bought was their 'Rivers of Babylon', with 'Brown Girl In The Ring' on the other side.

2FM, or Radio 2 as it was, started when I was quite young and my sisters listened all the time. In the early eighties we had *MT USA* on television with the late Vincent Hanley, a must in our house every Sunday. It had a huge influence on me, introducing me to Madonna (I'm still a huge fan) and we argued over who had the best video. Michael Jackson's 'Thriller' was at its height then, and he had amazing videos. *MT USA* was also responsible for Bruce Springsteen invading our house. His

Born In The USA album was played so often even my dad got to like it!

The first big gig I went to was The Waterboys in Kiltimagh. They'd had a number of hits by that time, like 'The Whole of the Moon' and 'Bang on the Ear'. I was meant to be studying for my Inter Cert, but me and a good lady friend (who was always up for a laugh and is still a good friend today) decided to go. Having no transport, and Kiltimagh a good fifteen miles away, we hitched a lift in a cattle truck. We had a great night, but 4am came with no sign of a lift. All the cars had gone, so in desperation I phoned my uncle to tell him we were stranded, knowing he would not be impressed by our escapade. Thankfully he got out of bed and drove to Kiltimagh and took us home. Our families thought we were in each other's house studying, and we had hoped to keep our little trip a secret. But it wasn't to be, and I didn't get to a gig for a long time after that. But The Waterboys were great and worth all the hassle, even if my Inter Cert results left a lot to be desired!

The first gig I played was with The Face Of February, a rock band in my local community centre in Kilmactigue, Aclare. We did covers of Guns N'Roses, Queen, U2, Bon Jovi etc. There were five or six of us and we practised for weeks in our sitting room with full drum kit, electric guitars, keyboards etc. The noise was deafening. I don't how my poor parents stuck it. I was so nervous beforehand, with family, relations and friends there in support. I was apprehensive about the music not being to the older generation's liking, but it was a great gig with a full house. That night lit the spark for me. As the show progressed I got more comfortable, and by the end I was on such a high I just knew it was what I wanted to do with my life.

Frustration can creep in, though, and all musicians have such moments. In the early years I often finished a gig after singing my heart out for three hours, and after paying the band I might have enough money for a bag of chips. Those times led to a lot of soul-searching about getting a 'proper' job. Luckily I had a very supportive family who helped me through lean times. After my accident I again questioned whether I should continue, but the messages I received from fans made me determined to get back on the road.

By far the greatest moments in my career were performing in Carnegie Hall in New York twice, the first time as the pinnacle in my first tour of the USA and Canada. My nerves were shattered, but I remember every minute. The second time was when I was better able to take in the magnitude of it, although I was still shaking like a leaf beforehand. It's such an awesome venue and I feel privileged to have sung there.

On the home front, a gig in the Olympia in 1999 will always remain very special. It was my first gig after my car accident. The reception I got will live with me forever. I felt so fortunate to be back doing what I love best when it could have been over. The standing ovation I got that night will always be special to me."

FAVOURITE ARTIST:
I like many different types of music, and I go through
phases. At the moment I'm into Delta Goodrum, Daniel
Beddingfield, David Gray and Robbie Williams. Barbra
Streisand and Frank Sinatra would also be top of my list.

FAVOURITE ALBUM:
Counting Crows' *August And Everything After*.

FAVOURITE SONG: 'Bad' by U2

74

WESTLIFE
Mark Feehily

Sligo-born Mark Feehily is a member of the highly successful pop group Westlife. Formed in the late nineties their success is unprecedented. To date they have sold more then twelve million albums world-wide and their albums have delivered the band over 52 platinum awards in over 25 different counties. The group have also played to live audiences across the world, smashing box-office records while continuing to record and release highly successful albums. In 2002 they released their Greatest Hits album, *Unbreakable*, a remarkable feat, containing no fewer then 10 number one hit singles.

"My earliest memories of music are of when I was in playschool, I used to stand up on the table at school and do all these kind of party pieces and I distinctly remember singing Billy Joel's 'Uptown Girl'. It's a bit weird now when I think of it because we ended up releasing it as a

Westlife single. It used to be difficult enough to get me up but it used to be no problem getting me up to sing that song. That song and a few big music videos really influenced me and made me fall in love with music. Michael Jackson had a huge influence on me as a TV viewer. You could say I was introduced to music through TV. Michael Jackson kind of ruled; it was hard not to like music when his stuff was on the TV.

Grease also played a big influence on me getting up on stage. It led to my meeting Kian and Shane from Westlife. A friend of my dad's lent us loads of videos, way back when not many people had a video recorder. We rented out a video player and my cousin I think lent us a copy of *Grease*. From the very first second to the very last second I was absolutely blown away. I had never really seen a musical. It was quite amazing to see it, especially on TV.

The first proper gig I ever went to was Michael Jackson in the RDS. I had gone to see stuff in local theatres but when it comes to a 'star' level it just blew me away and everyone else who went to see it. By the end it was almost as if the whole entire crowd of I think it was 35,000 to 40,000 people, had their hands up in the air. It was a really weird experience, really.

When I look at our first performance, it was in a place called the Hawkswell Theatre. There's a massive difference between what we did then and what we do now. It might as well have been a million people in front of me when I was younger because it was very hard to get used to singing in front of people. It was fine in my bedroom; I used to sing the house down every night to the point where my family would get underneath the pillows to stop listening to me. When I got in front of a crowd it was very difficult at the start and to this day it is something that is not my strength.

I hate to sound like one of those clichés, "let's do it for the music and nothing else matters", but when it comes down to it

I never was the sort of person who would be a pin-up by any means, I'm not dissing myself in any way, I'm proud of who I am and all of that. I wasn't a Mr All-the-Girls-Love-Me sort of dancer, all about the clothes etc. I had a major love only for singing. I do all the clothes and that kind of stuff now because it's part of being in the band but it's not something that I was ever crazy about. I was never sitting in my room wishing one day that I would be famous; it was more that I would be a singer or a well known singer. That's what I would say to myself. I don't mind doing all of that, it's part of the whole thing, it's a part of Westlife and that's what a five-piece is about, a unity and we have to have some sort of a common image going on stage. It's the honest truth I got into it for the singing side.

I get asked quite a lot about my best moments in music and it's so difficult. We have had so many great memories, that there is literally no one time that I could pick. We have travelled around the world and there are hundreds of things individually that would have been enough to keep me happy. Things like working with Mariah Carey, meeting Stevie Wonder, even getting to go to a Prince gig, just stuff like that. All the albums sales, all the numbers 1s, it's collectively unbelievable."

75 JIMMY MacCARTHY

Jimmy MacCarthy is one of Ireland's most respected songwriters and performers. Indeed, he is arguably the Irish songwriter with the most songs recorded by other Irish performers. His impressive list of cover versions includes 'No Frontiers' and 'Katie' by Mary Black, 'Ride On' and 'Missing You' by Christy Moore and 'Ancient Rain' and 'Ride On ' by Mary Coughlan. Artists of the international calibre of The Corrs, Westlife and Rebecca Storm all continue to enjoy performing the fruits of Jimmy MacCarthy's labour. Throughout his career Jimmy has been glad to help emerging and young talent on the contemporary Irish music scene through his generous willingness to offer advice and information.

Here he offers an inspirational story that will have particular resonance for everyone who picks up this book:

THE WINDOW - AUTHOR UNKNOWN

Two men, both seriously ill, occupied the same hospital room. One man was allowed to sit up in his bed for an hour each afternoon to help drain the fluid from his lungs. His bed was next to the room's only window. The other man had to spend all his time flat on his back.

The men talked for hours on end. They spoke of their wives and families, their homes, their jobs, their involvement in the military service, where they had been on holiday.

Every afternoon when the man in the bed by the window could sit up, he would pass the time by describing to his room-mate all the things he could see outside the window.

The man in the other bed began to live for those one-hour periods where his world would be broadened and enlivened by all the activity and colour of the world outside.

The window overlooked a park with a lovely lake. Ducks and swans played on the water while children sailed their model boats. Young lovers walked arm-in-arm amidst flowers of every colour and a fine view of the city skyline could be seen in the distance.

As the man by the window described all this in exquisite detail, the man on the other side of the room would close his eyes and imagine the picturesque scene.

One warm afternoon the man by the window described a parade passing by. Although the other man couldn't hear the band - he could see it in his mind's eye as the gentleman by the window portrayed it with descriptive words.

Days and weeks passed. One morning, the day nurse arrived to bring water for their baths only to find the lifeless body of the man by the window, who had died peacefully in his sleep. She was saddened and called the hospital attendants to take the body away.

As soon as it seemed appropriate, the other man asked if he could be moved next to the window. The nurse was happy to make the switch, and after making sure he was comfortable, she left him alone.

Slowly, painfully, he propped himself up on one elbow to take his first look at the real world outside. He strained to slowly turn to look out the window beside the bed. It faced a blank wall.

The man asked the nurse what could have compelled his deceased room-mate who had described such wonderful things outside this window. The nurse responded that the man was blind and could not even see the wall. She said, "Perhaps he just wanted to encourage you."

Epilogue:
There is tremendous happiness to be found in making others happy, despite our own situations. Shared grief is half the sorrow, but happiness when shared, is doubled.

Signed: Adam at the window?

Ride on,

Jimmy

THE END